Steps to Success

Also by Charles Humphrey Muller:

Novels
A Slip in Time
Release of the Dove
An Elusive Sanctuary
Wheel of Destiny
Circle of Deceit (pen name Callum Gunn).
Ocean Rapture (with *Joanne Carolyn Muller*)
Spirit of Joy (with *Joanne Carolyn Muller*)
Laura's Secret (with Elsie M. Young)

Non-Fiction
Waipori Reflections
Touched by Angels
Bragleenbeg Reflections
The Christian Teachings of Charles Kingsley
Fiction Studies: Victorian and Modern (McGraw-Hill, 1982)
Practical English Handbook, ed. C.H. Muller (McGraw-Hill, 1982).
Emily Brontë, *Wuthering Heights*, eds. Charles & Joanne Muller (Cape Town: Maskew Miller-Longmans, 1982).
Seven Studies in the Victorian Novel, ed. C.H. Muller (University of South Africa Press, 1982).
Unisa Studies in the Modern Novel, ed. C.H. Muller (University of South Africa Press, 1982).
The Fundamentals of Style in Written Teletuition (University of South Africa Press, 1983).
Workbook of Practical Criticism (Oxford University Press, 1983).
Explorations in the Novel, ed. C.H. Muller (Macmillan, 1984).
Study Guide for English Skills (Macmillan, 1984). (Co-authored with R.W.H. Holland.)
Dynamic English (Johannesburg: Juta & Co., 1988). Editor & co-author.
Charles Kingsley: Victorian Christian with a Modern Message (University of the North, 1979). (Inaugural lecture.)
Two Sermons of Charles Kingsley (University of the North, 1979). (Series A.)

Poetry
Worlds Apart: Poems of Contrast (with Beth Richards)

Steps to Success

A Testimony of Faith and Achievement

by

Charles Humphrey Muller
MA (Wales)   PhD (London)   DLitt (OFS)   DEd (SA)

DIADEM BOOKS

Published by Diadem Books

For information, please contact:

Diadem Books
8 South Green Drive
Airth
Falkirk
FK2 8JP
Scotland UK

www.diadembooks.com

ISBN: 978-0-244-39926-9

To have faith is to be sure of the things
we hope for, to be certain of the things
we cannot see.

(Hebrews 11:1)

Table of Contents

Introduction   1

STEP ONE: Visualising a clear goal   3

STEP TWO: Working out a strategy   11

STEP THREE: Seeking and finding - using faith   21

STEP FOUR: Tapping into the spirit   33

STEP FIVE: Letting go to grow   45

STEP SIX: Seeing beyond the visible   58

STEP SEVEN: Reaching out!   69

EPILOGUE   88

Appendix: A Tarnished Cup in the Attic   108

About the Author   113

Note from the Author

This book, *Steps to Success*, was first published by iUniverse in June, 2000, under the title *Have Anything You Really Really Want*. It is being republished under the new title since the previous iUniverse edition (including a number of other books I published with iUniverse) was, without my permission, assigned to an African author who was able to infiltrate and take over my iUniverse account. I have on numerous occasions asked the present owners of iUniverse (Author Solutions) to correct this, but without success. The previous edition, published under my own name, received excellent reviews, which can still be read in Amazon.

Charles Humphrey Muller
MA (Wales), PhD (London), DEd (SA), DLitt (UFS)

Foreword

Joanne with the Rolls Royce Silver Shadow the author acquired during his sabbatical year in Scotland in 1984.

Steps to Success: A Testimony of Faith is intended to be a thought-provoking study about the power of positive thinking and the Christian faith. It follows my own personal journey of faith and discovery as it describes how my Christian faith unleashed a positive power – in the attainment of personal, even material goals (including the acquisition of university degrees and a Rolls Royce!), but more significantly in the realisation of far-reaching goals: the discovery of my wife and ultimately the transition from university professor in South Africa to hotel-owner in Scotland. An important lesson in the experience of mid-life change is seen in the close dependence on God's love and boundless supply for all needs, material and spiritual.

From establishing an objective, working out a strategy, and using faith and initiative, this detailed thesis hopefully explores the essential principles for personal success and achievement and will guide the reader step-by step through the practical process of attaining goals. In the final analysis, however, the account asks whether it is the individual, or the invisible hand of Providence, which engineers the success – even to the extent of *changing* one's original goals, and changing one in the process.

CHM

Preface

Professor Muller has written a timeless guide on how to pray for personal success and achievement which is biblically based, but within and dependent on the will of God for each of us as an individual. It comes from a deep Christian faith, which he explores progressively in the course of the book as it matures and deepens. It is easy to read, which may at first mask the deeper meaning – a refreshing approach which will endear it to many. It has plenty of sensible, wholesome advice regarding how, exactly, he makes the prayers his own – personal but good sound psychological precepts for prayer, as taught by Our Lord.

He sets it as a story, a memoir of his own and his wife's experiences in the earlier part of his life, and in their life together. Indeed, it is in part autobiography and love story, of his upbringing in South Africa and his eventual meeting and marriage to Jo. Many will be able to identify with their struggles to bring up a family and the financial hardships of those early years together. I particularly admired the account of how he defied the negativity of his school teachers to attain, eventually, several higher degrees and academic success as a Professor of English in South Africa.

Some might deplore the seeming frivolity of not just asking God for a large, expensive car, but for a specific make and model, even for the exact colour and fittings! But this is an integral part of the process of focusing and longing that fuels the prayers. There is a lively humour in the account which disarms such potential criticism. This is not a manual of how God rewards the Christian with worldly riches and leaves the poor behind as undeserving. On the contrary, it is very evident that this focus and determination, even obsession, facilitated a tremendous amount of hard work and self-sacrifice from them both. Yes, God rewarded their prayers but they never lose sight of His will, in which 'we are justified by Faith alone'. For them God often seems to say, 'Not yet' or even 'No!' and they accept that His mysterious bounty remains His, to bestow or withhold according to his wider plan for each of us, but they continue to pray with intense yearning.

There is indeed an understated but clear spiritual progression in the course of the book which is very moving. The longing for worldly things gives way gradually to a recognition of a greater longing for

God's own presence as sufficient. The author's earlier acquisitions of degrees, a big car, houses and even a hotel, with all they symbolise for him and the family, become part of a progressive, deeper call. These things themselves become simply a symbol of God's everlasting bounty, so that we go on this spiritual journey with the author, and can see those successful prayers as no more and no less than a sign from the God who loves us that He will always listen and give and reveal His love to us in every possible way, till we get the message fully and the signs are no longer necessary.

There are hints as to how to deal with relative disappointment and failure, but the emphasis is, rightly, on the perseverance needed and the courage to go on asking. I find that there are some Christian books which lighten my spirits on this difficult path of God's calling – and a few which make me feel depressingly inadequate. *Steps to Success* is firmly in the first category. I came out of it laughing in pleasure and feeling very reassured about my place in God's world – which is as it should be.

Elinor Kapp
MB.BS [Lond] DPM FRCPsych. BA [hons]

Introduction

THIS LITTLE BOOK is more than a 'how to succeed' manual! It's a personal testimony, bearing witness to how my Christian faith opened doors and released the power of God – a God who loves and cares, who guides us to fulfil the special plan he has for each one of us.

On one level, it explores the essential principles for personal success and achievement. It's a record of how these principles worked for me. How did I achieve my three university doctorates? How did I apply myself, what research methods did I use? On a superficial, materialistic plane, how did I acquire my Rolls Royce, or my hotel in Scotland?

More important, how did I reach out and grasp a dream – a dream which, while I lived in Apartheid South Africa, seemed impossible? The book is a record of survival in *change*. In mid-life, to forego, to *let go*, all one's securities – a comfortable five-bedroomed home, a secure professorial salary and status, the Rolls Royce and other possessions – to reach out for an intangible, as yet unrealised vision of a life of spiritual satisfaction and service halfway across the world, certainly involves stress and crisis.

There are many who, in mid-life, find their old life cloying and unsatisfying. A change of direction at this time, possibly into self-employment, can be traumatic, to say the least. But to venture and establish a closer, trusting partnership with the Creator, is to achieve boundless satisfaction. It may allow the Creator an opportunity to release his power and reveal his special plan for you.

The book was written in two parts. Steps One to Six were written in England, after I had embarked on my journey of faith and discovery. The final step (Step Seven) and Epilogue were written *after* the successful attainment of my dream – a hotel in Scotland. At the conclusion of Step Six I was still unsure and uncertain, and had reached a stage where a new dream had unfolded and had to be visualised and hoped for. The final section shows how a persevering trust in God's promises and providence brought me home, and how God requires a practical application of faith – a faith which, metaphorically, may require one to walk on water!

God is as real today as he was when he spoke to Moses in a burning bush or parted the Red Sea to lead the Israelites across dry land. His power is as real today, and just as available to us, as when Jesus turned water to wine, walked on water, and appeared to Paul on the road to Damascus in a blinding revelation of his divine purpose.

Today we *do* have extra-biblical proof of God's miraculous reality and power. My testimony in Step Four ('Tapping into the Spirit Dimension') is an example of such evidence. There was nothing more special about me than others that I should have been blessed with such evidence – apart from my special condition of need at the time: for a moment, God placed me into his intensive care, enveloping me with an outpouring of his love. He loves us all equally, though he may extend some special care to the lost sheep, just as we might take extra trouble to find a lost coin.

My prayer is that God will use this little book to reassure you of his abiding and abounding love and care, and of his ever-present guidance in working out his special plan for you. May it help you to tap into the Spirit dimension and realise the dream God has implanted into *your* heart!

CHM

STEP ONE

VISUALISING A CLEAR GOAL

A **GOAL** is vital for any kind of success! You must have a goal, or, to use the scientific term, an *objective.*

And it *is* the first step. I've proved it. It's the foundation upon which all your actions – all your consequent actions – will be established. It's the first ingredient of a magic formula. There's no magic about it, of course – it just *works* like magic. It's the first step that unleashes – or begins to unleash – a creative force available to every and any human being.

You've heard of Jesus's words about faith: 'If you have faith like a grain of mustard seed, nothing shall be impossible to you!' (Matthew 17:20).

It's absolutely true. Faith is belief, and belief is based on something concrete – something clearly visualised – like that mustard seed. This metaphor of a mustard seed implies something that can be seen and touched and handled.

You must know what you want – and then you must VISUALISE it! You must identify your goal and see it clearly in your mind – in your imagination.

That's the way I got everything I have – my university degrees and three doctorates, the various houses I have owned in prosperous residential suburbs, my Rolls-Royce Silver Shadow, my professorship and headship of an English Department at a University, and – yes, believe it or not, even my wife!

And yet my English teacher once, in desperation, advised me to leave school. 'For heaven's sake, Muller,' he shouted, 'go to the Tech where you can learn to do things with your *hands,* for you'll *never* do anything with your brain!' (You can read about this again in the Appendix to this book.)

I was in the penultimate year of school, then. I was certainly heading for failure, since my previous report had about four red circles around my various subject averages. Mathematics was one subject where the average was always circled in red. I think it was my English teacher's remark that shook me. I realised I would fail Standard 9 – as the penultimate year of senior schooling was called in South Africa.

So, I dropped maths. I took commerce instead – an easy subject because it depended simply on learning facts. Then I put my shoulder to the wheel, and, by the skin of my teeth, passed Standard 9 – with no red circles in the final report. But this meant I no longer had mathematics as a subject, and it also meant I wouldn't be able to go to University: in South Africa, matriculation with exemption – permission to go on to University – was dependent on having mathematics or a third language in your final Standard 10 year.

And I had no third language – and now no mathematics.

And yet – I visualised myself at University! I saw myself enrolling. I saw myself attending lectures. I saw the letters 'B.A.' – Bachelor of Arts – behind my name. It had already become part of the reality of my future. Since one's life is a continuum in time, in a sense I already recognised that I *had* a B.A. degree. And so my strategy for obtaining the degree fell into line. Clearly I had to have mathematics as one of my final matriculation subjects. The strategy was almost automatic: I saved up my pocket money and enrolled for a correspondence course in matriculation mathematics. *And I didn't tell anybody!* That's an important rule. I kept visualising the B.A. degree, and that fired me with the enthusiasm – the *will* – to keep at my correspondence lessons. I conducted each lesson like a furtive love affair. I secretly cherished the desire for the degree, and this made the factors, the figures, the fractions, the geometrical theorems, take on a new appeal. And when the day came to write the matriculation examination, my schoolmates were surprised to see me in the examination hall. Instead of writing seven subjects, I wrote eight, for mathematics was an extra.

All this paved the way for a very joyful experience – the culmination of success. This happened on the day the results were released. The results were printed in a government gazette. There was quite a hoard of anxious matriculants around the city hall where the results were released, and I clutched my copy of the gazette with as much excitement and trepidation as anyone there. I looked for my name, and for the little asterisk that would indicate I could be admitted to University. My name *was* there – and the asterisk was there. I felt heady with relief and triumph! 'Charlie, did you pass *maths*?' someone asked. My old maths master was lounging on the city hall steps. 'Muller, did *you* pass maths?' he asked, with a wry grin. 'Oh yes,' I said, proudly.

My mother was equally impressed – so much so that she reimbursed me the pocket money I had spent on the correspondence course.

I had visualised, even dreamt, of passing, and of the ultimate reward of the degree – so much so that I could hardly have failed. Yet, as it happened, I only *just* passed mathematics – but the minimum average which I obtained served its intended purpose. It opened the doorway to University.

I had even daydreamt of passing mathematics. I relished, in my mind, the surprised looks on the faces of my peers, on the face of the maths master, and on the face of the English master: and I saw all of those surprised looks on that successful day!

I had visualised success. And I got success.

I think my acquisition of a Rolls Royce motorcar will best illustrate the power of goal-visualisation. I had heard before about this power. A member of my local Methodist church, one Sunday morning, told me about it. 'If you want a Mercedes Benz,' he said, 'you've not only got to ask the Lord for one; you've got to ask for a *specific* model and colour!'

I thought it would be very wrong to ask the Lord for something so materialistic! 'I hardly think,' I said, 'that that would be right!'

'Well,' he said, 'it's just to illustrate an important rule when you pray for something. If a Mercedes is something you really want, you've a right to pray about it. If it's God's will for you, he will give it to you. But if you do ask the Lord for a Mercedes – to come back to my example – you've *got* to be specific. You've got to specify the model, the colour, the horsepower, the upholstery, the steering-wheel padding, and so on. After all, you wouldn't just walk into a shop and say "I want a Mercedes", would you? You've got to order a specific model and specify what you want. It's like going to an estate agent for a house. You don't just ask for a house. You've got to describe the house you want – four bedrooms, a study, air-conditioning, where situated, price range, and so forth.'

It was years later, only after I had become a Professor of English, that I recalled my friend's words. Only then did I dare to aspire to something so materialistic as a luxury motorcar! Well, I didn't want a Mercedes, I thought. As a boy, I had always been aware of Rolls-Royce cars as fanciful wonders beyond my wildest dreams. To have and drive a *Rolls*, I thought, would really mean something. And I began to cherish a Rolls Royce car in my heart.

Of course, a professor's salary, even then, in 1982, was totally inadequate for saving up for a Rolls. The whole idea was madness. Nevertheless, I dared to ask the Lord, subject to his will!

I read Matthew 7:7 – 'Everyone who asks receives; he who seeks finds.' I had to ask and, the Bible told me, 'it will be given to you.'

'Well, Lord,' I prayed, 'I know this sounds ridiculous – but I know *you* know what's in my heart. If it's at all compatible with your will for me, Lord, may I find the means to have a Rolls Royce?' I must admit, it sounded very foolish and extravagant!

Then I remembered about being specific. So I bought books on Rolls-Royce cars. I looked at the advertisements in recent copies of *The Times* and the *Exchange and Mart*, and in motor magazines from England. I was then living in Pietersburg, in the northern Transvaal of South Africa, where Rolls-Royce cars were thin on the ground. I took a trip to Johannesburg where I saw a few second-hand models in a garage for exotic cars. The prices, even then, were the same as the prices for expensive houses! But I sat in those cars, smelt the leather, touched the steering wheels, and looked down the long tapering bonnets towards the little silver flying ladies – the Spirits of Ecstasy – at the end of those bonnets, and I felt what it must be like to own a Rolls.

Now I was in a position to be specific about what I wanted. I would have, I decided, a Silver Shadow, long-wheel base, gold in colour, with a gold-plated Spirit of Ecstasy, and with walnut picnic tables in the back. It would be a well-maintained second-hand model, of course – about a 1973 model, or later. And, half embarrassed by my audacity, I held up this vision to the Lord in prayer.

Now I would need a strategy. How – and where – would I acquire the car? The South African prices were ridiculous. The British prices looked more reasonable, but that would mean importing – and even then I would have to pay 100% duty on the original cost. Most people simply dropped the idea of importing a car – any car, let alone a Rolls – when they were confronted with the fact of the 100% import duty! In effect you had to pay *twice* the British price, as well as the shipping cost over and above that!

So I dropped the idea. But it resurfaced. It had gripped me. It wouldn't let me go.

So I worked out a strategy. Indeed, the strategy seemed to present itself as the obvious solution. I was due for my 12-months sabbatical leave. I arranged for my sabbatical leave in a year's time – in 1984 – and, in the meantime, I had a year to save up the British price, around £10,000 for a 1973 Silver-Shadow. According to South African law, I would have to purchase a car in the United Kingdom and use it there for at least six-months before being granted an import permit. So the leave would enable me to satisfy these conditions. I just hoped, of course, that I would have the import duty saved by the time I brought the car to South Africa at the end of 1984.

Every month, in 1983, I would have a target amount that *had* to be saved if I were to reach the target purchase price by the end of the year. I opened a special savings account. I took on extra teaching duties, lecturing for long hours in the hot humid climate of Venda University, nearly a hundred miles away – a distance I had to travel in afternoons and evenings twice a week. I let a cottage in my garden to receive extra income, too. Every month I met my target, somehow. And by the end of 1983, when I took my family to Scotland, I was able to put £11,000 into the local bank in Oban!

At that point my loving and ever-wise Yorkshire wife felt it would be unwise to spend all that money on a car, even if the car *was* a Rolls! The political situation in South Africa was deteriorating rapidly and, she said, having got all that money *out,* we should *keep* it out.

I agreed with her, and yet the idea of acquiring the Rolls, especially after all that visualisation and planning, wouldn't release me. Clearly what happens, when an idea is held for a long time, is that it *must* become a reality. I had been poring over manuals and books on the Silver Shadow for months – and my mind was thoroughly *conditioned* by the power of visualisation.

In another sense, I had asked the Lord for a specific Rolls, and it seemed downright rude if, at the eleventh hour, I turned down the gift! Or, if you like, my subconscious simply demanded the reward after all that beholding of the promised vision!

So I looked for my car, to see if it really existed. I saw only two ads for long-wheelbase Shadows – in London – and took the train to London accordingly. I phoned the first advertiser from my hotel. His car had been sold the day before! Long-wheelbase models were rare, it seemed, and soon went. I took the tube, then, to a garage in South-west London where the other car was. I got there only to be told that it had been sold! 'But,' said the salesman, 'we do have another long-wheelbase – a much prettier car, in my opinion.' He took me into the back of the garage where sleek Rolls-Royce bonnets were like a hypnotic power. And *there* – in shining, immaculate, unbelievable splendour – was my car! It was the very car I had visualised: gold, with gold-plated Spirit of Ecstasy, and a 1975 model – for sale, unbelievably, at £10,000! Only one thing – it didn't have picnic tables.

'Can picnic tables be fitted?' I asked, 'Say, for £500?'

'Certainly, if it means *that* much to you!' said the salesman.

So walnut picnic tables were fitted. Three weeks later I and my wife, three daughters and little son Angus took the overnight sleeper to London. We returned to Scotland in our own Rolls Royce car. Children waved at us from busses. In Scotland a policeman saluted me. When we reached the glen where we had our rented cottage, a retired and stiff-necked colonel, who had hitherto ignored our existence, nearly broke his neck running to open the gate! It was the most magnificent drive in my life!

At the end of 1984 we shipped the car to South Africa, by which time there was enough saved in my bank account to pay the 100% duty. We collected the car from the shipping agent in Cape Town and, again, enjoyed the magnificent 1000-mile drive to Pietersburg in the northern Transvaal. I was the only Rolls-Royce owner in Pietersburg, and practically in the whole of the northern Transvaal!

I have often thought back upon how the dream of that car was impossible to let go. I think it should present itself, not only as an example of the power of goal visualisation, but as a warning of just how deep or strong mind-conditioning can go. Be very sure, at the conception of a goal, that it's something you *really* want. Because, once implanted visually into your mind – with all of its specific details – it takes over and demands realisation. I felt, when I was presented with the choice of leaving the money in Britain, that I hadn't really got a choice. I had already chosen – or the goal had chosen me. It became an obsession. In fact – it *had* to be realised. I felt that if I didn't go ahead and buy the Rolls, after all the planning, that I would be incapable in future of ever realising or possessing a goal! I argued that I had to be true to myself. It might have been rationalisation – but I may have been right. At least the exercise reinforced in me the conviction that anything is really possible, if you really want it. It laid the foundation for future action and future success. It made me believe in the impossible dream.

Coupled with the power of visualisation, of course, is the power of prayer, which unleashes the power of the universe. But that is a subject for another chapter.

STEP TWO

WORKING OUT A STRATEGY

ONCE A CLEAR GOAL is conceived and visualised, a strategy for the realisation of the goal almost seems to present itself.

Why?

Because, if you want something badly enough, you'll find a way. Success depends not only on clear visualisation, but on powerful feeling. The power that really gets human beings going is emotive – feelings, or emotions. Your intellect, and the use of your intellect to plan, is necessary – but your intellect is worthless without the fuel that gets it going.

Your mind is like a fantastic machine, capable of tremendous resources; but it's useless without the fuel that powers it – emotion, or feeling, or enthusiasm.

Enthusiasm is the power that drives the human machine. The word *enthusiasm* is Greek and means 'to be possessed by a god.' Therefore, ardent or lively interest in your goal will be like divine possession! It won't let you go until you've realised your aim. If you've prayed for something, therefore, you've actually asked God to release his own possessive power! You've tapped into a real divine power – the very *source* of Power.

That's why we say 'where there's a will, there's a way.' A strategy will surely present itself if your emotive power is strong enough. In as much as you first have to switch on the electric power to make a vacuum cleaner function, you've got to switch on a power – your feelings and your will. It's like a steam engine. Without the steam that drives it, it's nothing more than a complex piece of engineering. So make sure you've switched on the power, or lighted the fire to make the steam to drive the machinery!

Clear visualisation helps to stoke the fire of enthusiasm. That's why daydreaming isn't altogether a wasteful activity. Your mind alights and dwells on what you really want. It's like making a wish. Have you wondered why so many wishes *do* come true? They come true because, in making the wish, you've visualised your goal. You've also focused your energy upon an objective. The detailed visualisation is the first step towards making it concrete. The Greek philosopher Plato said all reality is but a copy of the original idea that exists in the mind of God. We begin by picturing the *idea*.

Then the strategy falls into place. But if we think along scientific lines, we can organise and streamline our strategy. We can order it so that our progress towards the goal is systematic and accelerated. We submit our vision to the natural law of growth. Natural growth is something that takes place in progressive steps, one at a time. Achievement is always like that. Rome is never built in a day. But we can realise our dream or wish surprisingly quickly if we fix deadlines for the steps on the way.

I have written three doctoral theses and before that two masters' theses, as well as various academic textbooks. In each case the thesis or book would not have been completed if I hadn't fixed *deadlines* for each chapter.

My first academic supervisor, Professor Arthur Johnston, warned me about the dangers of not establishing deadlines. It was when I was working on my MA dissertation at the University College of Wales in Aberystwyth. He said he had known academics who had researched and read in libraries on their topics for *years*: they never felt they were ready to write, and in the end never wrote the thesis. Professor Johnston said he had himself read and researched for ten years at Oxford before writing his doctoral thesis. Since then I've seen it all myself – research students, and even university lecturers, who never get beyond their first degrees, and yet who renew their registration for a master's or doctoral degree every year. Every year they pay the expensive registration fee; every year they send letters to their supervisors to explain why they haven't submitted any chapters! Procrastination is surely the thief of time. The truth is, we seldom feel ready to act.

Jesus said to the lame man at the pool of Bethseda: 'Take up your bed and *walk.*' There comes a time when we have to take the initiative and act. Before Jesus said that, he asked the man an important question. He said, 'Do you *want* to walk?' The man replied, 'Yes' – and only then could he take the initiative.

We must have a positive and willing frame of mind before we can begin to achieve our goal. We have to *want* to walk! We must want to possess the goal badly enough. And then we must identify deadlines, or progressive steps, in our journey towards the goal. After each deadline we must take up our beds anew. Each time it will be easier. Each time we will be stronger and wiser. And each time we'll be nearer the goal! The power of God will come to us as we take that initiative at each step. The saying, 'God helps those who help themselves,' is full of wisdom.

It's like walking towards those closed glass doors you find at airports and departmental stores. The doors remain firmly closed until you step onto the plate or intercept the sensors that activate the mechanism that makes the doors slide open. God opens doors in the same way. He will never open a door at the time when you ask for a door to be opened. You must ask, of course. But having asked, you have to believe in him – and in yourself. You have to get up and walk in confidence towards the closed door. When you get there, the door will open.

In other words, each step must be made in faith. The Bible tells us, 'Without faith it is impossible to please God.' It's absolutely true. I've tested this principle many times. Faith and positive initiative – stepping out in confidence – is what pleases God. Only then will he open the doorway to your selected and visualised goal.

Often, of course, the path towards your selected goal is uphill. But growth is normally upwards! Growth follows a law of natural development – from one vantage point to another. When I wrote my thesis, I did more than set deadlines for the progressive chapters.[1]

I was methodical.

I asked myself, how many chapters do I want to write? Seven? Very well. Then I chose suitable and reasonable *deadlines*. I made those deadlines coincide with the end of university vacations, or periods of leave, or long weekends. I told myself that the research for each chapter should be completed by a week – perhaps two weeks – before the vacation, leave period, or long weekend began. This meant that I had to be *ready to write* a week or two before the vacation, leave or weekend break. This meant that I would have *time free* for the writing. I made sure that I didn't plan any other activities for those free times.

I made sure, in other words, that *preparation would coincide with opportunity*. All my research – my reading and note-taking – had to be completed by the writing deadline.

When the writing deadline arrived, I had to apply firm discipline. The whole family understood that I wasn't to be disturbed during my morning writing sessions at home. One of my little daughters understood this clearly and stuck a notice in her large scrawl on my study door: 'Don't disturb – daddy is WORKING.' I came to an understanding with myself that I would write at least three or four pages a day. It wasn't an impossible or very demanding

---

[1] One of my colleagues at the University of the North, impressed by my post-graduate degrees, once suggested that I write a book detailing how to write a thesis. What follows here is, in effect, is the result of that suggestion!

workload. And usually I'd write six or seven pages – and complete the chapter well before the end of the vacation or leave-period!

An important rule was always to allow time to relax and enjoy with the family. I used the carrot-at-the-end-of-the-stick incentive, too. Always be sure to reward yourself for work done! During leave periods which were my writing times, I would always be sure to leave the evenings free. A morning of successful work – of four or five pages written and edited – would always ensure that a long walk, or evening free with the family, was enjoyed to the full. A rest earned is a rest enjoyed! All I was doing – unconsciously, perhaps – was applying the principle of positive reinforcement which B F Skinner, the behavioural scientist, wrote about. Skinner discovered that rats learnt the routes through mazes a lot faster when they realised a reward of cheese would be found at the end of the maze!

The principle of positive reinforcement – or self-reward – was a lesson I learnt early on in my writing career. When I was a lonesome postgraduate student working on an MA dissertation at the University College of Wales in Aberystwyth, fish-and-chip shops were plentiful as a source of reasonably cheap meals. As a student of limited resources I survived, in those days, on fish and chips! But there was a Chinese restaurant, too. *There* was my means of celebration – of reward. I promised myself that, on the completion of each chapter, I would reward myself with an evening out at the Chinese restaurant. How I looked forward to those evenings! I would relish the pleasure of having another chapter complete and handed in to my supervisor. I would dress up and savour the Chinese meal – so different from fish and chips – with well-earned satisfaction. (I remember how, on taking out a cigarette – another pleasure reserved for the occasion – the Chinese waiter always jumped forward to light it for me. The sense of self-importance added to the satisfaction!)

At all times throughout the periods of research and writing I would, of course, constantly reinforce my purpose by visualising the goal. In my study at home, for example, I would leave a space on the wall where I would hang my next degree certificate. In short breaks between spurts of writing I would look up and imagine – visualise – the framed certificate hanging in its allotted space! (And I would be sure to hang it in that space after it was awarded!)

Each chapter of a thesis – or book – had to have its own strategy, of course. Many research students use a card-index system. It's a good system because notes on cards can be filed and interchanged in a shoe box! For me it was a somewhat different system that worked. I used a series of notebooks. Each notebook had its own contents. Take, for example, my research for my chapter on Wilkie Collins's novel *The Woman in White*, which formed the third chapter of my DLitt thesis *Drama and Melodrama in the Fiction of Wilkie Collins*. In a notebook labelled 'R' I copied notes taken from contemporary newspaper and magazine *reviews* of the novel. In a notebook labelled 'B', I copied relevant notes from *biographies* on Wilkie Collins. In notebook 'L' I collected extracts from *letters* written by Collins's contemporaries about him or his novels. Notebook 'C' would contain notes collected from *critical studies* on Collins – in this case, on *The Woman in White* in particular. And so forth. Then I would plan the chapter and use my own coding system of cross-references to the notebooks. I would have my skeletal plan, with headings and spaces, on a sheet of paper. This skeletal plan – the basic framework for the chapter – would look like this:

Notebooks:

R = Reviews

B = Bibliographies

L = Letters

C = Critiques

Skeletal Plan

Ch. III

The Woman in White:

Title: Melodramatic Incident and Dramatic Characterisation

Intro: Plot versus character in the Sensation Novel

R4 (S) R94 (Lytton on ch)

B44 (S)

C144 (Setting)

L18 (Plot)

R Reviewers' reception of the novel

R9 (chs subservient to plot) B5 (Ellis on ch)

R45 (atm) L9 (Lever on scene)

R88 (S & Setting) C7 (Quarterly: appeal of proximity)

M Melodramatic appeal

R66 (Plot & M) B44 (M) B6 (Ellis: no better melodramatic novel
in Eng lang)

R74 (Sat Review: ch) L5 (M)

R75 (Sat Review: Th) C11 (M, Th)

Th Theatrical effects

R26 (atm) C55 (Th)

R44 (Th) C64 (Th)

B2 (Dr) C74 (Des)

Motif The dead-alive motif

R26 C5 (Hyder - Th)

R68 (Times)

R62 (Sat R - atm)

Cont <u>Contemporary appeal: the romance of the here and now</u>

R22 R42 R48

Plot <u>Intricate plotting</u>

R42 (literary chessplayer) R63 (<u>Sat R</u> - 'mechanical' talent)

R68 (<u>Times</u> - serious flaw in plot)

Ch <u>Superiority of character portrayal: courtroom drama</u>

R28 (Marion) R48 (Marion) R29 (Fosco) R22 (Fosco)

R93 (Marion) B26 (Marion) R98 (Fosco)

B5 (Resourceful Heroine) C44 (Fosco - credible & worthy

antagonist)

K <u>Conclusion: dramatic, not melodramatic</u>

L27 (CD to WC)

C18 (TS Eliot : Bk dramatic because of 2 chs)

*   *   *

This is a very simple way of ordering and categorising the raw material. The headings indicate the main contents of the chapter and the main steps of the argument, beginning with the Introduction and ending with the Conclusion.

I made sure that between the headings I left enough spaces to fill in my cross-references to the notebooks. I would then work methodically through each notebook. If I found something in notebook 'R' (Reviews) that would be helpful to refer to in my Introduction, then I'd write in the cross reference to notebook 'R' under the first heading. Thus R4(S) would mean: See notebook R (Reviews), page 4, for a reviewer's remark on the Victorian Sensation novel. In the margin of the notebook on page 4 I would pencil in the code 'Intro', so I could spot the reference easily at the time of writing. (Naturally, I would be sure to number all the pages of the notebook.)

The word-symbols on the left-hand side of the Skeletal Plan (**Intro**, **R**, **M**, **Th**, etc) are the symbols I've pencilled in in the margins of the notebooks. In this way, as I said, I can quickly find the material to which I have referred in the heat of writing! You'll see that, after most cross-references, I've also used a very brief key word or word symbol (sometimes a short phrase), to jog my memory:

S = Sensation Novel; **Setting**; **Plot**; **atm** = atmospheric effects; **Th** = theatrical effects; **Dr** = dramatic technique; **Des** = descriptions or descriptive technique.

These keywords or symbols are very helpful when the actual writing begins. They help me to organise my argument.

For each chapter I may draw up three or four copies of the skeletal plan, each with a different set of references. I would always have a special 'skeletal plan' for the cross-references to Notebook 'N' – the notebook in which I've written notes on the novel itself (in this case *The Woman in White*). This notebook – Notebook 'N' (Novel) – would constitute my primary material. All the other notebooks constitute my research or secondary material.

I will have made the notes in Notebook 'N' (my primary material) while actually reading through the novel: always have a pencil or pen in hand while reading your primary material. Some of your best ideas come to you then and need to be jotted down at once! (Make sure that each note made here refers to the exact page in the novel or source book which you're reading and to which the note refers. These page references will be important when you compile the footnote references.)

The point I'm making, here, is that system is essential for success. It's part of the Scientific Method, the real basis of achievement. Science is *organised knowledge*. Its aim is the discovery of truth – not only in the world of material nature, but in the immaterial world of the mind. It's the basis, therefore, of achievement in any human endeavour – in science, in business, or in sport. In applying the scientific method in my DLitt chapter, I utilised a recognised and proven strategy. This strategy consists of three important steps:

1. A getting together of all the necessary facts;

2. A classification of these facts; and

3. An effort to arrive at their meaning by using the principles of logical reasoning.

In my chapter this strategy was organised into a *framework*, or a plan. This framework, or plan, was my formula for success. **Step 1** was achieved through my reading and research; **step 2** was achieved by my system of notebooks linked by the cross-references in the skeletal plan; and **step 3** was achieved at the time of writing the chapter. The writing came easily as a result of the preceding steps.

In the achievement of any goal, or objective, your strategy is your framework and your formula for success – the means, or the route, which you must follow.

When I wrote my DLitt chapter, this formula of a step-by-step strategy, with set deadlines, was the scientific method in microcosm. When I planned my financial route towards the acquisition of my Rolls Royce, it was the same method in macrocosm.

In either case the principle was the same. In either case progress was fired by enthusiasm - real desire. In either case this desire was sustained by the clear and detailed visualisation of a *specific objective.*

STEP THREE

SEEKING AND FINDING:
USING FAITH AND INITIATIVE!

THE BOEING 747 banked as it began its descent towards Heathrow.

I watched as the clouds thinned and streamed past the little window and over the metal wing. Far below the green fields began to show through. Then I was watching the familiar rows of red terraced houses. It had been seven years since I'd looked out on the same view. It had been receding, then, as I returned to South Africa with my PhD from the University of London.

In all that time – though I was now 35 years of age and a senior lecturer at a university – I had never found the right woman whom I could make a life-companion. So I had given fate a push – and the first of three computer dates was waiting to meet me at the airport!

The aircraft shuddered under the decelerating effect of the wing flaps. I watched the raindrops spray off the wing as it cut into the damp London sky.

Yes, I thought with amusement, it was certainly a strange thing for a conservative academic to do. It was the start of my sabbatical leave and I was coming to Britain to further my research on distance education. An intervening month would be spent at a few American institutions.

What, indeed, would my academic colleagues say if they knew I was about to be met by a computer-selected date? Well, I thought defensively, I *had* gone about the whole business like a serious researcher. I had filled in the computer questionnaire very strictly. I had eliminated from choice the selection of women who, in the slightest way, failed to come up to the ideal I had in mind. After all, I had very specifically visualised my goal!

I must admit that I was impressed by the detailed nature of the questionnaire. I could specify qualities like home-loving, the kind of house I wanted her to like (a country cottage instead of a penthouse flat or town house), and the kind of music she should enjoy. A tailor-made woman, in short! There was even a block that specified what my – and her – favourite pet was – a cat, hound, goldfish, and so on: criteria that could be matched for common factors!

Of course, the combination of sociological, psychological and personality information wasn't aimed to provide a match based on maximum similarity of character and tastes. Needs and interests that complemented one another constituted the real basis of compatibility. And a compatible match, Compudate explained, 'is a pair of people who have a high probability of being mutually attracted.'

That meant, I thought with rising excitement, that the woman waiting for me at that moment in the airport's arrival lounge was – for me – a near-perfect woman! She would be a country-loving, gentle person who liked to travel, who enjoyed the theatre and liked literature. A girl who liked children, who was a good cook, was not more than five feet and eight inches tall and not less than five feet and five inches short, who was slender and who considered herself attractive. And – who *didn't* smoke. (I had dropped smoking some years before and felt very virtuous about it.) She will have attended a private school, would have a good sense of humour, and – most important – would be conservative, refined, and a good Christian.

I remembered how amused my friend Bob had been when I showed him my completed questionnaire. 'Good heavens,' he exclaimed, 'you're going to get Margaret Thatcher!'

'Not at all,' I replied with equal amusement. The whole thing, for me, was a kind of adventure – an interlude of fun – yet I half believed in it. My remarks were made half in jest as I entered into the spirit of the game. 'The computer,' I said, 'is supposed to search its memory files for a woman that best complements me. Don't you see? She'll be the other half of the quince!'

'*Quince?*' His eyebrows drew together in puzzlement.

'Yes,' I explained. 'The ancient Greeks believed we were once sexless – a perfect whole, like a quince. But the gods cut up the quinces into male and female pairs, and since then we've got hopelessly mixed up. We spend the rest of our lives searching for our other halves. The computer narrows down the search.'

'But *look* at this!' Bob slapped the form. '*Your* bit of quince will be tall and skinny, all stretched into nothing. I mean, five feet eight inches and only eight and half stone!'

'Of course,' I heard myself telling Bob, 'she must have the golden key.'

'Golden *what?*'

I smiled. 'I mean, that magic *something* that makes you fall in love.'

My friend's eyebrows arched in disbelief. 'And you expect a *computer* to find that for you!'

The aircraft shuddered as it hit the tarmac. Airport buildings loomed outside, grey and shapeless in the rain.

She was in there, somewhere, I thought, and some of the words from Compudate's literature ran through my head: 'I've met the girl of my dreams through Compudate... a match that couldn't have been made better in heaven... our compatibility is almost uncanny... your microchips have done it again!'

Patricia. That's how I had addressed her in her letters. She replied in her characteristically bouncy style: 'I'm *not* Patricia. That's far too sophisticated. I'm *Pat*. You'll see, when you meet me!'

Pat was really going to be fun. Her style was lively, her personality bubbly. And she'd insisted on coming to the airport to meet me. 'I'm going to run up and kiss you, right away!' she wrote.

She had been the last of four names on the computer printout. A computer run normally produced six names with addresses and telephone numbers, but my strict selection of criteria had severely limited the range of the memory banks! I'd written the same first letter to each of the women, telling them (tongue in cheek!) how carefully they'd been selected. It omitted nothing of importance, informing the selected and elected candidates even of my commitment to Christ, my involvement in lay preaching, and of my university degrees. To say the least, the letter was presumptuous!

Only two of the women replied – Pat, from the south of England, and Hilda, from the north of Wales. I paid £5 for a second run, this time adjusting only one criterion: I cancelled my elimination of non-smoking women, and received a second printout with six more names. All these received the same letter, and out of these only *one* replied – a very unlikely candidate ten years younger than me: Jo, in North Yorkshire, who warned me one could only expect to find someone one could 'gel' with if one were completely honest in filling out the form.

My presumption arose partly from my religious faith. The whole endeavour was done in the spirit of fun, as I said. And yet, I had no objection to leaving the door open for the Lord's guidance. If anything, I've always been an opportunist. So, I invited the Lord to use this opportunity to help me find the ideal partner. Why not? Jesus said, 'Ask, and you shall receive.' Just how literally could we take his words?

Of course, the Lord would take into consideration that my own choice factors were already in the pages of the completed questionnaire. But hadn't he said himself, 'Seek and ye shall find?' Clearly, he expected one to take one's own initiative. In effect, I was going to walk towards those closed doors of opportunity. If they opened for me when I reached them – and if I found myself really *wanting* to go through! – then, surely, the doors would slide open.

I knew, naturally, that a computer couldn't select a woman with what I called the golden key. But I felt pleased I had prayed. It made the adventure all the more exciting because now I had really committed myself to something that was more than a game. It was like having signed an agreement. It was daring and therefore, perhaps, exciting – and dangerous! Did I *really* want a marriage partner? Be *careful* when you pray! The Lord looks deep into the heart. If he sees an earnest desire there – a visualised goal – he's bound to take you seriously!

He certainly took *me* seriously.

But I didn't think so when I met Pat!

She flounced towards me as I emerged from customs, implanting a kiss on my cheek like the passing lick of a puppy.

'Hello!' she said in an accent that rang oddly in my ears. 'Told yer ah'd kiss yer, din' ah?!'

My reflex smile was like the outward mask of happiness.

I took in her soft milk-white skin, her rich auburn hair, the flecks of gold in her smiling brown eyes. And I took in her more than ample figure. The red slacks did nothing to diminish the impression of size, stretched around sturdy thighs and ending in flared bottoms.

'Hello, Pat,' I said as my mental vision of her dissolved. I added insincerely: 'Nice to see you.'

Though I spent a week seeing Pat – out of politeness – I had, in fact, eliminated her from that moment of meeting her at the airport. I really don't want to be unkind to her. Naturally, I'm not using her real name. And I'm sure that, by now, she has made someone a wonderful and loving wife. After all, she was a super cook. She was a bank clerk, and stored and catalogued all her pre-prepared meals, ticking off each one with meticulous care when she removed it from the freezer. She was incredibly organised. When we left for a picnic outing, she would remember everything, including the keys for the car I had rented, and the picnic would be packed with love and precision.

When I brought myself to tell her I would be moving on, she was heartbroken.

'What am I doing *wrong?*' she asked tearfully.

How could I tell her she didn't have the golden key?

She was trying too hard, perhaps. She was possessive and I felt smothered by her. Watching television with her on the sofa, I had felt quite compressed by her larger-than-life presence.

In some measure, I thought, Pat *did* complement me in a statistical sort of way. I was an absent-minded academic, out of touch with reality, while she was a practical, down-to-earth homemaker. In many respects the computer had come up trumps. She could cook, she could sew, and she was forever cheerful and went into raptures about babies. She was a ready-made housewife. And she didn't smoke.

Yet it was patently obvious she hadn't been very strict in filling out the questionnaire! She was hardly the tall scarecrow Bob predicted I would find!

A research project in the United States intervened and it was only after a month that I had the opportunity to look up Hilda in North Wales. And it was clear, from the outset, that she *had* been strictly honest about the details she confided to the computer.

She was the most elegant scarecrow I'd ever seen. No, I mean this quite sincerely. At five feet and eight inches, she was tall, and just short of thin. She made her own clothes and looked charmingly elegant in whatever she wore. She had her own house. Her antique furniture and tidy home radiated exquisite taste. She didn't smoke, of course. With her soft and sad eyes, she was a little self-effacing. She was also so gentle and so caring – a district nurse, and a lovely Christian. I'll always remember how, when we went to her village church together, she spent a long time on her knees praying. I felt she was praying for me. In retrospect I wonder, now, if she was an angel. She radiated peace.

I've never understood why I didn't fall in love with her. After all, she *exactly* matched all the details I'd specified. I recall how pleasantly surprised I was when she drew up in her little red car – when I glimpsed her gentle face framed by a mass of auburn hair. When she got out of the car I saw she was slender, very tall – perhaps a little ungainly – but immaculately dressed in a pale yellow wool suit. 'I'm a Welsh leek, you see,' she smiled. 'Long and thin!'

She was home-loving, too. The following evening I watched her with admiration as she prepared supper in her compact kitchen.

'Here,' she said, handing me a bowl and a whisk. 'Perhaps you could whisk this into some nice fluffy cream?'

'Certainly,' I said, and took the bowl to the worktop.

'Watch it doesn't turn into butter, now,' she lilted, smiling.

I watched her as I whisked the cream. I recalled how meticulously she pronounced the Welsh names as she drove me through the countryside, getting me to repeat the names and correcting me gently if I mispronounced them! As I whisked the cream I saw her again, in the church, on her knees, her auburn hair falling forward and over the high collar of her blouse. She looked thin and vulnerable, and my heart went out to her.

'How's it going?' she asked musically. Her faraway eyes smiled as she looked at me through the strands of her hair.

'Oh... yes.' My mind came back to my task. I looked into the bowl and there were lumpy yellow specks in the turgid texture of the cream. 'Well, I don't know. I think you'd better look at this.'

She came over. She looked taller than ever in a brown skirt and blouse that emphasised her slender figure.

'Oh!' she gasped when she looked into the bowl. She put her hand to her mouth, her knees sagging a little under the effect of amusement. 'I've never actually *seen* anyone turn cream into butter. How did you do it?'

'You know, I'm not really fussy,' I apologised.

'Well,' she said, testing the thick mixture with her finger, 'it was supposed to float on top of the Irish coffee. If you don't mind it sinking to the bottom...' She smiled as she looked askance at me.

It's a moment that has remained with me – her relaxed manner and gentle sense of fun.

She would have made a superb companion. Though I was unaware of anything like a golden key, she was pleasant to be with. I might even have revisited her, had I not gone on to North Yorkshire and met Jo.

I might as well, I thought. After all, I had gone to the trouble of that second printout! So I took the train to Harrogate where I booked into a guest house just across Montpellier gardens where Jo shared a flat with three other girls. She was a secretary and, unlike Pat and Hilda, didn't have her own house. But then, she was only twenty-five. Pat and Hilda had both reached thirty.

I knew that Jo couldn't fit my visualised ideal. For one thing, with the only letter I had received from her, she had enclosed a photograph of herself. It revealed a willowy girl in jeans seated on a motorcycle. The dark glasses she wore obliterated the eyes. She was hardly the helpmeet for an academic.

Nevertheless, I must confess, she was the girl that intrigued me most. There was something about her letter – a lively style with a bright and quick sense of humour. When I phoned her from London to arrange the date for meeting her, I was intrigued by the laughter that rippled through her speech. The Yorkshire accent was just detectable.

I felt I needed to impress this young lady. I made reservations for dinner at the Old Swan in Harrogate. No expenses spared. At least I would enjoy the evening.

It was dark when she emerged from the door of her flat. I was aware of long straight hair with a nose that pointed through it, and a tall body with willowy arms ending in tapering fingers. 'Do you like curry?' she asked briskly. I said yes, but I'd booked a table at the Old Swan – and at once found myself marching vigorously to keep up with her long loose strides. We circumnavigated the Rolls Royce parked in the front of the hotel and before long were seated in one of the bar lounges.

'Do you really have a motorcycle?' I asked her.

'No!' She dug into her handbag and extracted a packet of cigarettes. 'In the photo I sent you I was posing on someone else's. But I *do* have a sewing machine.'

This was my first clear picture of her – lighting a cigarette and exhaling smoke. It went with her image of sophistication: the high cheek bones, the arched brows, the nonchalant smile. I took in the long dark hair, the snug-fitting black blouse and floral skirt. She had an air of a woman of the world. I distinctly remember thinking she was very attractive, in her worldly way, and an impossible catch for a fuddy-duddy like me.

'You must have a swarm of handsome young men after you,' I ventured. 'I'm amazed you're still single, even at twenty-five!'

'Oh,' she laughed, flicking her hair back. 'I'll never get married. There's so much to do.' She laughed. 'I didn't join Compudate for marriage, you know. I wanted a fresh range of friends.'

A warning? Or was it the old hard-to-get game?

All I know is that, by the end of the evening, I had fallen in love with her. The mere contact of her lips, when I kissed her goodnight, made my head spin. Her breath was smoky sweet from the cigarettes. All at once the ground dissolved. I fell and fell, through fathoms of space. Then I was dimly aware of her fingertips on my chest, pressuring my away, gently.

'Goodnight.' She smiled her amused smile.

I had found the golden key!

She turned out to be everything I was seeking, in spite of my first reaction. She is certainly home-loving. She has been a wonderful mother to our children. She is understanding, gentle, yet independent, too. She doesn't smoke anymore, either. And she is a devoted Christian, having accepted the Lord as her saviour.

Indeed, she proved to be a perfect 'helpmeet.' In everything we did, we worked together. We wrote two novels in which we collaborated as authors. In running our hotel in the Scottish Borders, we worked as a team. We were either constantly talking to each other, or simply being sustained by each other's silent presence.

The Lord, as I said, looks deep into the heart. When you pray, he detects your real desires and your real needs. He answers in spirit and in love. As Jesus said, when you ask your father for food, he doesn't give you a stone or a snake! (Matt. 7:9-11.) He knows what's best for you, even before you ask. And he'll see through all your words to the picture held in your heart.

I had visualised a goal. That goal had become deeply embedded in my subconscious. That's why, for me, Jo had the golden key even though, at first, I didn't realise it. She had the physical and personality specifications that fitted my ideal. Subconsciously, if not consciously, I was seeking, and seeking for a specific ideal. How often, when we meet our partner, we say, 'I feel I've known you all my life!' In a sense, we've already conditioned ourselves for that woman – or that man – before we've met her, or him. And the Lord knows it. Seek, and you shall find your heart's desire!

The Lord will confirm this desire. After I met Jo, I had to come to a decision very quickly. I was due to return to South Africa within two weeks! I remember walking through Wolloton Park in Nottingham, a few days after meeting her. Finding my ideal had come so suddenly. Surely it was madness to ask her to marry me after just meeting her! I was bewildered, too, that I hadn't fallen in love with a more conservative and more likely ideal like Hilda in Wales. I looked deep into my heart.

'Lord,' I prayed, with deep yearning. 'It's *Jo* I want. Please let me have Jo, Lord!'

And then a wind swept through the park and the trees around me shook like crazy! It was like the mighty force of the Lord's spirit blowing around me and I felt his answer in my heart: *'If that's what you want, she's yours.'*

I felt my heart would burst with joy and I ran all the way back to the hotel where I was staying. I phoned Jo and she agreed to see me again.

Before I returned to South Africa in September we attended the Methodist church in Harrogate. It was Harvest Festival. The whole church was bedecked with flowers and fruit. As we sang the hymns, we held hands. And then we were parted until February, when I met Jo at the airport at Johannesburg. We drove down to East London in the Eastern Cape, and we attended the Methodist church service on Sunday evening. Again, it was Harvest Festival! The whole church was bedecked with fruit and flowers, just like the church in England had been when we last worshipped together! My heart was moved and I thrilled at the knowledge of the Lord's voice in my spirit: *'You are each other's harvest!'*

I hope I've conveyed something of the magic and wonder of our computer-assisted meeting. It was magical and wonderful only because we had taken a positive initiative – even if that initiative was in the subconscious! For me it's evidence of the power of clear goal visualisation combined with the power of faith. It might be cynical to say nothing wonderful ever comes to us out of the blue. It rarely does. Wonders happen – but usually we have to go forward, sometimes towards doors that appear closed, to find them, and have them happen to us.

STEP FOUR

TAPPING INTO THE SPIRIT

Come near to God, and He
will come near to you.
(James 4:8)

ABOUT 4 **A.M**. on the 28th of November, 1984, I had a
strange and wonderful experience. In essence, I told God I
loved him – and to my amazement, he answered me and told me
he loved me.

That was it, in a nutshell; but the experience was so shattering I
don't think I'll ever be the same. I've told people it was like an
extra-terrestrial experience, because I had never experienced
anything like it before. However, before I go into details about it,
I'll need to say something about the events that led up to it. The
experience, you see, came as the climax of a year of seeking and
doubt.

I suppose I'd always felt there would be something special about
1984. Perhaps it was because of George Orwell's novel *Nineteen
Eighty-Four*! But it was special for me because it was my
sabbatical year. My previous sabbatical leave was seven years
earlier in 1977, the year I met Jo. This time it meant a whole year
off from the university in South Africa where I was employed as
Professor of English. At last, I would be able to complete my
long-cherished book on the Christian teachings of Charles
Kingsley, the Victorian novelist. But it also meant that, in the
acres of free time, I would be able to finish writing my novel

based on the second-coming of Christ. It was a novel I was writing with Jo, and we had decided to call it *Rapture at Sea.* (Now republished as *Ocean Rapture.* In the book Jesus is seen to come back early one morning while a ship is crossing the stormy waters of the Bay of Biscay; imagine the consternation of the passengers when they discover all the Christian passengers have vanished!)

At any rate, writing a novel would be a refreshing change to writing academic articles and textbooks. In a way, I had had a surfeit of academic writing, with eight published textbooks and three doctorates behind me. Much of it had been for my own glory, and I felt I had never fulfilled my real purpose for the privilege of being in this world – to proclaim God's word and his glory.

There was another aspect of the year which had little to do with glorifying God. It was the year when I acquired my Rolls-Royce motorcar. As I've said, I had long cherished the notion of acquiring what people term 'the best car in the world.' Well, why not? I had worked hard, writing textbooks, and had travelled repeatedly to the tropical outposts of my university to lecture in conditions of sweltering heat. But at heart, of course, I was seeking a cherished desire.

And so, for various reasons, I chose to spend the year in Britain. Jo is British and she longed to spend time in a setting that was green and exhilarating like the Yorkshire dales where she had roamed free as a child. We needed a secluded spot for our writing. And, of course, Britain was the home of many Rolls-Royce cars.

We found the perfect place: a cottage at the head of a secluded glen just south of Oban in Scotland. In the winter it was a bleak glen and Scammerdale loch looked forbidding with its dark waters, waves ridging across the surface as the wind whined around us. The cottage was warm and cosy with its oil-fired central heating. The windows gave panoramic views of the loch, fringed by the Christmas pines and mountains that opened to the amorphous sky. We watched the snow settling on the mountain tops while the rain filtered down gently, soaking everything. The cottage was like a life-support capsule, a micro-world set in this wonderful yet alien environment of cold, snow and drizzle. We observed the world in safety, like seeing the landscape of a strange planet from the security of our capsule.

'It's lovely,' Jo said. She looked wistful, her deep brown eyes raised to the powdered peaks above.

'It *is* bleak, though.' I looked up at the sky. 'Look how dull it is.'

'Yes, but the atmosphere is tremendous.' She frowned. 'It's dull, yet the sky retains light. There's a feeling of hope and contentment. Listen to the wind. There's music in it.'

'That moaning noise!' I laughed.

'No, I like it. The place has a feeling of warmth, of home.' She smiled. 'Perhaps this is as close to heaven as I'll get on earth.' Then she turned to me, concern in her eyes. 'You know, I don't want this year to pass. It holds my future, somehow.'

I suppose, in a sense, it did hold her future. If our writing partnership proved successful, it meant the possibility of writing full time and settling in Britain where she most wanted to live. Somehow she sensed, I think, that I wasn't altogether with her in spirit. I wanted to write a novel, yes – but there was the Rolls Royce, too, and that meant taking all our British money back with us to South Africa. For me, the Rolls Royce was like a golden calf and demanded a sacrifice.

Looking back, the year was full of vivid impressions. It turned out we had chosen the worst winter in twenty years. The snow fell and fell and heaped up in drifts a few feet thick. One day Angus, the farmer next door, came churning up to the cottage in his four-wheel drive. The school car with our young children in it hadn't returned, and the snowstorm was turning into a blizzard with winds over 70 mph. We found the car, all right, bogged down in a drift next to the loch. The little faces of the children were white and anxious as they peered through the windows, but relieved to see us.

The gale swirled the snow around us as we dug around the tyres. Our hands grew numb and our movements sluggish. I felt like a man of soaked cardboard pretending to dig. The shovel weighed a ton and around me was the swirling white, blinding to look at. The frightening thing about a blizzard is that the whole world 'whites out.' If I stepped more than a few feet away from the car I could see nothing at all – just blinding whiteness.

The car and the children were safely rescued, at any rate. But the memory of the occasion lingers with me, like a lesson. It reminds me that we can't step too far back from Jesus, or we'll lose sight of him. We would be swamped by chaos. Somehow we have to keep him in sight, and our eyes on him. Just like Peter walking on the water: as long as he kept his eyes on Jesus and not on the waves around him, he didn't sink.

My most vivid impression, of course, was acquiring the Rolls Royce. (One doesn't 'buy' a Rolls, a salesman in Glasgow told me: one 'acquires' one.) It was magnificent, of course, long and sleek in gold over walnut. The children were quite enthralled, being driven out of London in such a magnificent dream machine. Yet this was one experience I could have done without. Even the Saturday traffic in London was heavy, and I kept losing my way as I tried to find the M1 out of London. (This was before the invention of SatNav!) I was terribly tense manoeuvring so expensive a piece of technology through unknown streets of speeding vehicles. I was barely in the right frame of mind to thrill at the superb handling, the gliding motion, the finger-sensitive steering, the silent and powerful thrust of the engine as it propelled us into traffic streams. But at last we surged into the freedom of the motorway, relaxing as we adjusted our seats for maximum comfort, feeling ourselves lift and tilt as little electric motors hummed discreetly. For a moment I was transported –

more than literally, I mean! The realities were cushioned and translated into a new 'spirit' existence. The wet windscreen, the wipers moving intermittently, insulated me from a world that was familiar but distanced.

It was fun, for a while, owning a Rolls Royce. It was difficult to justify, though, and I tried to see it as an unavoidable part of my destiny. In a way, I had made it a part of my destiny, of course. In March I wrote in my diary:

Destiny is irresistible, and may seem illogical. It seems illogical for me now – at this point in my life – to buy (I mean acquire!) a Rolls Royce. But there it is – it demands obedience and expression now. The Rolls Royce from henceforth is a vital expression of my life. To avoid it is to ignore an obsession, and that would damage my creativity.

But, really, I was feeling more than a little guilty for having spent so much money on a personal ambition. And it wasn't long before a certain dryness of heart set in.

I felt a need to get closer to the Lord. The novel was finished and by the summer had already been rejected twice by publishers. Jo and I began our next novel, which we called *Spirit of Ecstasy* after the Rolls-Royce mascot. (This novel, now published as *Spirit of Joy*, was a romance and featured the Rolls in the story; but it was really about an academic who, like myself, feels dissatisfied with life and misguidedly buys a Rolls Royce in search of spiritual fulfilment.)

I began to climb up into the hill above the cottage to seek more guidance from God. I found a tree growing out of a slope, and the trunk was looped to form a perfect seat. Sitting there, overlooking the loch, now an expanse of deep blue set amongst soft green slopes, I felt close to God. The breeze caressed the leaves above me and the white dots of sheep on the slopes added to the tranquillity of these moments. There I sat, reading daily from Psalm 104, about God who 'makes the clouds his chariot' and 'walks upon the wings of the wind.' The evidence of what I was reading was all around me. I had once discovered this third verse of Psalm 104 on a stone plaque in the Valley Gardens in Harrogate, in 1977. It had given me comfort then, and soon afterwards I had had that marvellous experience of divine reassurance in the wind sweeping through the trees in Wolloton Park. So now, again, I was seeking comfort – and reassurance.

'Dear Lord,' I prayed. 'Use our writing to your Glory. That's all that I really want. Publish our novels, and I will use them as a platform for preaching your Gospel.'

Was it a kind of a bargain with God? In any case, he ignored these prayers. The manuscript of *Rapture at Sea* kept coming back from publishers. The theme was too esoteric or way-out, they said.

Eventually I became fed up. Jo could no longer help me write, either, since she was having trouble with her eye. She had got a seed stuck in her cornea, but our doctor in Oban thought it was an infection. He kept prescribing ointments and the problem persisted for three months. Eventually the impediment was removed at the hospital in Glasgow. Nevertheless, before then, the sense of darkness and failure grew stronger, in spite of a beautiful summer.

'Dear Lord,' I prayed. 'Please heal Jo's eye. And don't forget the novel.'

But he remained silent. The summer slipped by and the sense of failure increased.

'The whole year is a waste of time,' I said bitterly, one day, as we sat beside the stream that fed the loch.

'How can you say that?' Jo squinted at me through her dark glasses. Because of her eye she couldn't stand the light.

'Time is supposed to be growing short before the Lord returns. How can we spread the Gospel if we can't find a publisher?'

'You're so impatient.' Jo waded into the stream, keeping her face turned away from the sun as she tried to catch a minnow. She was enjoying Scotland, in spite of her eye. 'We have to serve our apprenticeship first. People don't publish their first novels.'

But in spite of her sensible advice, I grew angry with the Lord. He seemed to ignore my prayers. What was the point of going up into the mountain? The year was drawing in, in any case, and it grew colder and windy again. Soon I stopped speaking to the Lord altogether. I didn't bother with the Bible, either. I got on with my Kingsley project, visiting universities and libraries in the south. I barely gave the Lord a thought.

One dark night I felt particularly depressed. The year had almost completely wasted away, and all I had to show for it was a Rolls Royce that gave me little satisfaction. I walked out into the night and once again spoke to the Lord.

'Lord,' I said, leaning on the cold metal of a farm gate. 'Frankly, I don't think you're there.'

I felt idiotic, speaking into what I knew was a void.

'I don't feel anything, God.' I listened to the stillness of the night, hoping there would be some sign of his presence.

Some dark shapes moved in front of me, restlessly, and I caught my breath. But they were just cows. I felt cheated, spending all this time writing novels for his glory. What did he care?

'In fact, God, I... I don't think you really care.' I grew more daring. 'In fact, I don't think you really exist.' It was the first honest prayer I had prayed for a long time. 'I don't *feel* anything. Surely, in your great power, you could make me feel something, if you cared?' It was a challenge, I suppose. I listened, trying to feel something. But there was nothing. I was praying into a vacuum.

'Anyway, God, I'll go on talking to you. Just in case you *are* there.'

I listened again. This time... yes, this time I *did* hear something. It was like soft footsteps in the night. The grass rustled nearby. I held my breath. Had he really heard me?

The grass near my feet moved and a black cat slunk past me. It disappeared into the night.

I felt drained and flat. 'You see, God,' I said, 'I even hoped that cat was you.' I turned away and walked disconsolately back to the cottage.

Just after that a book arrived unexpectedly from Ruth and John, Christian friends living in Cape Town. The book was *Nine o' clock in the Morning* by Dennis Bennett. I threw it aside when I saw it was about the work of the Holy Spirit. Later, however, I began to dip into it, and found that Bennett frequently asked the Lord for small things – and got answers, too. If he wanted a dry day for a picnic, for instance, he would ask the Lord to stop the rain from falling in the picnic spot he planned to use; *and* he would find, when he got there, that it was the only spot for miles where it *w*asn't raining.

That was odd, I thought. And yet, if the Lord really cared, he *would* show his concern in small things.

So I thought I would ask for silly things, too – things which nevertheless mattered to me.

One of the things that was on my mind was a new stainless steel exhaust system I wanted fitted to the Rolls Royce before it was shipped to South Africa. I had arranged with a small specialist in Yorkshire to do the job on a certain Monday a week before the shipping date. It was the only day he could do the job, but he warned me that he couldn't do it if it rained. He was good at supplying and fitting new exhausts, but had to do it in a yard where there was no cover. 'I'll have to arrange for a dry day, in that case,' I said.

So I approached God again. 'Lord,' I said, 'I know this is very silly. But I do need to have that exhaust fitted on Monday. And you know I can't afford the more expensive garages. Could I have a dry day on Monday? Just in Boroughbridge, that is. You can let it rain everywhere else.'

When Sunday came and we were driving the Rolls southwards to Yorkshire, there was a disturbing smell of burning mingled with the sumptuous aroma of leather. I couldn't locate it, and I eventually asked the Lord to show me where it was coming from. At once smoke appeared from under Jo's seat and she gave a shout of surprise. I stopped the car and found the old exhaust had developed a hole and was blasting hot gasses up at the floor of the car, baking the carpet! I telephoned the Automobile Association from the next service stop and they were on the spot at once. They flattened a beer can and wrapped it around the pipe. This must have been the first time a Rolls was patched with a beer can!

The next day, of course, was my appointment in Boroughbridge in Yorkshire. I found the place on the Sunday evening in the rain, just to make sure I knew where to go the next day. I found the man and said, 'It's raining.' He said, yes, the forecast was bad for the whole week, but he told me to bring the car to him the next day anyway: he would just have to cope.

The next day dawned and the leaden clouds hung ominously in the sky. But for the whole day, not one drop fell! And the new exhaust system was fitted expertly.

Two days later I had another appointment, this time in Luton near London for a new windscreen. (I wanted a tinted windscreen fitted before shipping the car.) There had been forecasts of serious fog. The week before there had been a terrible pileup on the motorway due to fog. 'Please Lord,' I prayed, 'I'd rather not have fog.' When the day came the winter sun shone brilliantly on the motorway. I put on the radio of the car, just in time to catch the announcer's warning: '...motorists to drive with extreme care in the terrible weather at present lashing the country...' *What* terrible weather? The day was calm and the sun was actually being a nuisance!

So I came, eventually, to accept that it didn't matter about *feeling* in one's relationship with God.

'The Lord is a FACT,' I said to Jo. 'His presence is a fact. He is real and unquestionably *there*. That's all that matters.'

'Yes.' Jo looked at me with amusement. She had been to Glasgow hospital by this time and had had the speck in her eye removed, so she could look at me with both eyes. 'But one should feel God's existence, too.'

'No,' I insisted. 'Feeling doesn't matter. It's enough that he exists!'

It was important, of course, that each day I was getting one step closer to God. I was spending more time in prayer, again, because now I knew he was listening – even if I didn't feel anything.

Just after that I was alone in London for a final visit to the British Library. The car had been shipped and in two weeks we would all be on our flight back to South Africa. It was the 27th of November and a British Council friend kindly put me up in his London home. He gave me a comfortable bed in a tiny room at the top of his house. I was hardly prepared for the incredible surprise in store for me.

It was about four the next morning when I woke up with some asthma. I turned over and lay on my back when I became aware of a woman seated beside my bed. I ought to have jumped out of my skin, especially since she radiated a soft light! But the strange thing was I wasn't in the least bit frightened. On the contrary, there was an immense sense of peace and warmth and contentment. And, I *knew* her – or, I should say, it was as though my spirit recognised her. Yet I couldn't put a name to her. It didn't matter. It was enough that she was there. She was elderly, and I felt afterwards she was like an old German teacher I was very fond of as a child. But afterwards (and this is very strange, for I don't understand it) I felt she was like Corrie ten Boom: that name came to me very clearly, afterwards, yet at the time I had never read any of her books. In any case, the sense of warmth and comfort made me want to pray. I lay back and said, simply: 'God, I love you.'

That was when it happened. All at once there was a flood of light from above: a sudden downpour, like an energy beam of pure power and pure love. It came straight down, like a pillar from heaven: but it was a stream of heavenly power, like electricity that surged through me, like a waterfall pouring, rushing through me.

I knew it was God. It was overwhelming. I felt like a small child on the breast of its father, held ever so tightly. I was crying and sobbing helplessly, overcome with joy. Somehow it was my spirit that was crying, not my physical body. I was held in a firm grip: movement was impossible. I had closed my eyes, and now I dared to open them for a moment: the room was flooded with light! A vague human form stood by the bed. I felt fear, now, yet total acceptance by God: it was too much for me to stand for long. I wish I'd had the courage to surrender totally to the accepting love of God. And I felt so unworthy, so ashamed, in spite of the total acceptance by God. Perhaps that's why I cried: 'Oh, please, please let my life be worth something to you!' And yet no demand was being made on me. At that instant, very powerfully, I felt the sentences in my mind, wordlessly, like a telepathic force: *'It's all right. You don't have to justify yourself or do anything to make me love you or want you.'*

Then suddenly it was all over.

But as I thought, 'It's over,' and while I still felt elated from the experience, I was aware of a desk standing in the room. It was a visual impression, of course, but the physical reality of the desk was uncanny and lucid. It was a modern desk, tall and narrow, like a pulpit. It felt inviting. I knew then that my calling was to write – to proclaim God's word and message of love through the written word. As if to confirm this, the thought pressed into my mind: *'Feed my lambs.'*

And then, finally, there was a feeling, like a chuckle, as though God were saying, 'Did you say feeling didn't matter?'

That was years ago, but I still ask, 'Did it really happen?' Of course, I know it did. I've been blessed with more than biblical proof that God lives and that he loves me too! For some time after the experience I had an overwhelming sense of love for everyone that I never had before.

Since then I've read Corrie ten Boom's *Tramp for the Lord*. She describes a similar experience of the Lord's presence – when she was healed in hospital. In a sense, I was healed, too. God goes to the sinners and failures, and I was failing badly.

It was this experience of tapping into the dimension of the spirit – of drawing nearer to God, as the Apostle writes in James 4:8 – that made me sell the Rolls after I had shipped it to South Africa. It led to the most difficult step in the adventure of achievement – *letting go to grow*.

STEP FIVE

LETTING GO TO GROW

SO FAR I've spoken about four important steps in achieving one's goal:

1. Visualising a clear objective

2. Working out a strategy

3. Using initiative

4. Drawing near to God

These steps release certain kinds of power; they are, in the same order,

1. The power of direction

2. The power of planning

3. The power of daring

4. The power of the spirit

The four kinds of power synthesise, of course, as long as the objective is clearly conceived and visualised, in the first place. The combined power doesn't necessarily come, however, from taking the steps sequentially. This is because drawing near to God will release the spirit power at any stage of your life. The spirit power of God is the most transforming and the most dynamic power you can ever tap into.

'Seek ye first the kingdom of God,' Jesus says, 'and then all these things will be added to you.' God, who knows our needs in the first place, will supply our material needs – and help us towards our goal – once we have our priorities right. Seeking God's Kingdom is the first priority. Therefore, in effect, what I have labelled as Step 4 should be Step 1. I have simply made it Step 4 here because that has been the order of my personal growth. How much faster my growth would have been had I got my priorities right from the beginning – and put God first in the first place!

But then, it often happens that we *do* draw much nearer to God at a later stage of growth. Growth can be a haphazard process, at first, taking wrong turns before we find the right direction. That's why, when I drew closer to God, I found I had to let go many of my realised material goals before I could grow further. Jesus tells us he is the gardener and that often he has to prune us. Many of the unfruitful branches he has to cut off are those branches in our lives that grew when we went after immature goals. These earlier goals may even have been realised with God's blessing – like my Rolls Royce. It's possible that, at the time, I needed to realise it. It taught me a lesson about achievement. A young girl will learn the same lesson when she aspires to an expensive doll, and a small boy who aspires to a train set. Those goals were right for that girl, or boy, at the time. They are goals the Lord will bless. There comes a time, however, when we have to put away childish things.

My first three steps, then, are relevant to the materialistic plane; but they are also relevant to the immaterial plane, as I demonstrated in using initiative, or daring, to find the girl of my dreams!

The step of drawing nearer to God is relevant to the immaterial or spiritual plane. Nevertheless, as I said, drawing close to God and the unleashing of prayer power is also important in the material sphere – for God cares for *all* our needs. 'Look at the birds of the air,' Jesus says, 'they don't sow or reap or store away in barns, and yet your heavenly father feeds them.' And then Jesus asks:

'Aren't you much more valuable than they?' And then he tells us to have God's kingdom and his righteousness as our first goal, and all material needs – food, clothing – will be given to us as well. (You'll find all this in the sixth chapter of Matthew. It's a lovely exhortation on why we shouldn't be weighed down with material or financial worries.)

Perhaps it shouldn't be surprising that as we draw nearer to God, and He draws nearer to us, our material goals will become less important to us. Indeed, as I found out after possessing my Rolls Royce, there was a certain dryness of heart. Material goals, like pretty clothes, jewellery, extravagant cars, prestigious houses and swimming pools, have a limited ability to satisfy.

Why?

Because we are essentially spiritual beings. We are created by God, who is a Spirit. And the more we develop our higher, or spiritual powers, the less appeal the material will have for us.

Material goals, once realised, can be frustrating. For one thing, they're so awfully subject to decay or damage! Whenever I used to take out my Rolls, I was a heap of anxieties! The sheer expense of having to replace or repair would be exorbitant, especially in South Africa where all the parts would have to be imported. I remember one of my first outings in the Rolls in Pietersburg (now renamed Polokwane). I participated in an exotic car meeting. My car attracted all the attention. I drove with rare Mercedes and Cadillacs in what the owners of the cars called a 'brag parade.' Then I drove home. A bus came in the opposite direction and threw up a stone. The stone cracked my windscreen. I felt the crack go right through my soul!

There was my sparkling swimming pool, too. I was a slave to that pool. I rarely had the pleasure of swimming in it. All my time was spent cleaning it. It was a ceaseless battle of years against algae.

'Where your treasure is, there your heart will be,' Jesus says. My expensive home, my swimming pool, my Rolls Royce, were important to me. They took up a lot of my time. I spent time cleaning the Rolls, admiring the way the gold came up bright every time. It was a golden calf.

But I had already had that powerful spiritual awakening in London – and these material assets were less and less able to satisfy.

And the material things were keeping back my growth.

So, over three years, I sold everything.

Letting go was the most difficult thing I ever did.

But I had to do it. At the time, just months after being back in South Africa, we were also terribly aware of the desperate plight of the country.

As a member of the white privileged class, I was one of many who had big houses with swimming pools, and expensive cars. I had two other cars, apart from my Rolls and my caravan. And yet, there were thousands of black people who lived in shacks. The Group Areas Act forced them to live in impoverished townships some twenty miles outside the prosperous white cities. They had to travel daily on overcrowded busses to work in those cities. The servant women had to leave at 4 or 5 a.m. every day to get to work in time.

There was the constant barrage of foreign news reports, critical of this situation, relayed on our television. One felt defensive. As one of the beneficiaries of the apartheid regime, I had much to lose if there were to be a revolution. I also felt terribly guilty. I used to argue: 'But I didn't invent apartheid. I don't support it. It wasn't my fault, being born white in South Africa.' And yet I enjoyed the benefits, the privileges, of being white. Perhaps it was only natural to aspire to material things. After all, people did this in California, or London, and no one pointed fingers at *them*.

Nevertheless, it wasn't easy to live with my conscience – a conscience conditioned by the news and criticisms from abroad. If I continued to live in South Africa, I continued to live with an uneasy conscience.

You could say this made it easier, for me, to let go. Much easier. Especially when, daily, the situation was worsening. Cars were being stoned on the roads. Bombs were going off at supermarkets and post offices. Conservative black people and even some whites were being burnt alive by means of the 'necklace' – a burning tyre doused in diesel oil placed around the neck of the victim. It got to the point when Jo was frightened to go into town to do the shopping. There was an air of a national uprising. The university where I worked became, in effect, a military camp, with army vehicles trundling across the campus. One had to be checked in and out, at the gates, by soldiers bearing guns.

Nevertheless, letting go the old things is not easy. But it's necessary for change. We can't grow without changing. And we can't change without letting go.

In our hearts we knew we had to change our circumstances. After the year spent in Britain, writing together, and especially after my experience of the Lord's loving spirit in London, we had an urgent desire to move to Britain. We felt it was the Lord's will for us. In her book *Beyond Ourselves* Catherine Marshall said that often what the Lord wants for us is what he puts into our hearts. In other words, if you look into your heart, to your deepest desires, you may find the very will of God for you. Sometimes I have prayed, 'Dear Lord, put hooks in my heart. Change my will to *your* will.'

And so we came to recognise our deep yearning to move to Britain as the Lord's will for us.

But how could we move to Britain without having a specific goal? Getting a job there, as an academic, would be well-nigh impossible. We were well aware of all the stringent academic cutbacks imposed by Maggie Thatcher's government. Professors and lecturers my age – 43 – were being retired with golden handshakes, not employed.

Nevertheless, as a starting point, we conceived a visualised goal – an unpretentious but modern four-bedroomed house in Harrogate, where Jo's parents lived.

And so we put up our house in Pietersburg for sale. We had barely completed building on an impressive bedroom extension overlooking the swimming pool, and we were very comfortable. It felt crazy to sell. In England we could never afford anything remotely as comfortable, or as spacious and large. For one thing, the exchange rate was rapidly deteriorating. Had we moved to Britain at the end of 1983, when we went on my sabbatical leave to Scotland, my capital would have been twice as much. This is why so many South Africans, who had built up their capital in the country, refused to move. They had too much to lose.

By then, too, the South African government had introduced what they called the 'financial rand'. If one emigrated, one was allowed to take out Rl00,000 as a family – *after* the money had been converted to the financial rand. Now, the financial rand, compared to the normal – or commercial rand – was worthless! In effect, you gave your life's savings away to the reserve bank of South Africa. And so, anyone emigrating with Rl00,000 in financial rand would arrive in Britain with less than £l4,000! In most parts of the United Kingdom that wouldn't have bought a one-bedroom flat. So, in effect, the financial rand kept many white South Africans in South Africa – or their money in South Africa, even if they did leave.

It takes a great deal of courage to let go. But, then, as I said, there was the increasingly intolerable South African situation. Also, there was the dryness in my heart when I faced the prospect of staying – of holding on to my professorship and to my material things. But most of all, there were the hooks in my heart – hooks which, we surmised, and hoped, the Lord had put there.

When prospective buyers came to look at the house, there was always the inevitable question: 'Why are you selling?' And Jo would reply: 'The Lord has told us to sell.' The reply caused a number of odd looks.

It was important that we had visualised a clear goal in the small modern house in Harrogate, for this gave us our interim direction. After that, we would have to go on to the next goal, not yet conceived or revealed. In this we were depending a great deal on the Lord's guidance. We knew he wanted us in Britain. We didn't know exactly, yet, where – and for what purpose. All I knew was that I had a calling – to write, and in doing so 'to feed his lambs.'

And so, in letting go, we would be depending on divine guidance, moving, perhaps, from goal to goal. This is another principle of providence mentioned by Catherine Marshall in her book *Beyond Ourselves*. She calls it 'sailing under sealed orders.' In the Second World War ships often sailed under sealed orders. When they reached certain geographical locations, the orders were unsealed. Only then did the ship go on to its secret destination. It was like that with us. We identified, in our hearts, our interim goal – of letting go and going to England. We were confident that when we reached certain co-ordinates in time and space, the Lord would reveal the next goal.

It took nearly three years before the house was sold. Property values were falling sharply because of the country's state of emergency. In all that time we held on to our vision.

Persistence, or endurance, we learnt again, were important facts in realising a goal. Once you have a clearly visualised goal, *hang on to it!* Never underestimate the power of tenacity!

Jo visited her parents in England, in the meantime, and looked at houses in Harrogate that were like the one we had visualised. She came back with lots of sale particulars. This helped us to visualise our house there more clearly. It also focused our purpose. We were able to fortify our minds – and our intentions – by occasionally looking at the now vivid mental picture of our four-bedroomed house in England. It's the mind, after all, in its unconscious energies that does the work in making a visualised goal materialise – in making a dream come true. There is a great deal of power in the practice of autosuggestion. Repeatedly looking at the picture in our minds, and talking about it, was a kind of self-drill in willpower. Irresolution will undermine and decay one's purpose and vision. Therefore we kept praying about our goal, confirming our desire to live in England. We believed in the mind-law that every thought, persistently held, tends to become an action. Persistently held, our house in England would become a reality. We had implanted our vision, and repeatedly reinforced it.

And yet, the house in South Africa remained unsold and apparently unsaleable. We kept reducing the price. At length we were prepared to accept offers that were less than those we had turned down a year ago.

Then Jo suggested re-mortgaging the house. If we re-mortgaged, then at least we'd have released some money to transmit to England in the meantime.

And then, I thought, I'd better face up to selling the Rolls. I was putting that off till the last moment. But if I could sell it, then that would release more money to transmit in the meantime.

This, at least, would be taking *the initiative.* It would be acting in faith that the house *would* be sold, and that avenues for transmitting the money to England *would* be opened. It was showing the Lord that we believed the closed doors would slide open when we reached them. It was putting our money where our mouth was!

So, with a heavy heart, I took the Rolls to Johannesburg to sell it. I remember how I prayed for strength of will while I unlocked the metal gates of my driveway before sunrise. It certainly took courage, too – to part with a long-cherished possession – a result of an ambition that had become a reality through dreams and endurance.

I drove that beautiful dream machine with its sleek golden bonnet through the silence of the pre-dawn. It travelled smoothly and silently, and I felt like an owner about to betray a faithful and beloved thoroughbred. I took the car to a garage that specialised in Rolls-Royce cars. Here I gave it the last service I could give it. Then, while waiting for the service to finish, I phoned the president of the Rolls-Royce Club of South Africa. Which of two showrooms would he recommend for selling the car?

'Paul,' I said. 'I'm here in Jo'burg. I'm going to sell the old girl.'

'*What!* Not your Shadow?'

'Yes.'

'Will you bring the car to my office first? I want to see it again.'

'I'm not driving her through the Jo'burg traffic, Paul.'

There was a silence. 'Do you know where the zoo is?'

'Yes.'

'Meet me there, then. At the main gates.'

When the car was ready I drove it to the zoo. Paul was there. He drove the Rolls round the block.

'I'll give you R64,000 for the car,' Paul offered.

When I arrived home that night, it was without the Rolls and Paul's cheque for R64,000 in my pocket. I had made a clear profit of R20,000!

The Lord had made it easy for me, I thought. The transaction had been as quick and painless as possible.

It was as easy to re-mortgage the house. When I filled in the application form at the Building Society, the lady helping me said, 'You won't get it, you know.'

'Oh?' I said, looking up.

'Do you want me to submit this application anyway?' she asked.

'Yes,' I replied.

'Well, there's no harm in trying,' she said.

Four days later a clerk phoned me from the Building Society. 'Where do you want us to deposit the money?' he asked.

And almost immediately avenues opened for sending commercial rands to England! A British Council friend was returning to England and was willing for me to use his special allowance as a foreign visitor. Another good British friend whose salary was paid in England welcomed the opportunity of simply exchanging salary cheques with me. Apart from that, there was the normal annual allowance of R6000 a year that each South African resident was allowed for overseas visits – which, of course, we used on each of our annual trips to England.

And as soon as our available funds were nearly all transferred, the house was sold!

Jo and I visited England together in Easter 1987 for two weeks and looked at houses for sale in Harrogate. At that time only just a little more than half our capital was in England, so our plan was simply to *look* at houses for sale. We saw a few and saw one that was just like our visualised ideal – a neat four-bedroomed house with long-distance views of open country, for sale at £50,000. 'We want to get one just like that,' I said. 'I only hope the prices won't have gone up too much by the time we get the rest of the money over at the end of the year.'

On the last day of our visit I thought we might just visit a couple of building societies. 'At least the managers will know us when we look for a mortgage when we come over next time.' We planned to buy a house by the end of the year when we expected to have all of our capital in England.

We went into the Woolwich Building Society and the manager was absolutely charming. 'If you want to buy a house now, I'll give you the money,' he said. 'Have you seen anything you like?'

I was aghast.

'But I only have £24,000 in England at present. And my job's in South Africa.'

'No matter,' he said, unperturbed. 'With money like that, you're a good risk. Can you comfortably manage a monthly mortgage payment of £250 at the present?'

'Easily!

Half an hour later we walked into the estate agent and bought the house with the enchanting open views.

Fifteen minutes later we were seated in a restaurant celebrating over coffee. We had a total sense of unreality and disbelief. It was a dream come true! There are times when one has to wait upon the Lord. But when it's time to act you have to act fast. I felt in my spirit, while listening to the manager of the building society, that it *was* time to act. The door had slid open. And I went through, rejoicing.

I had let go in South Africa, and now I had a house in North Yorkshire!

We shipped our furniture in August. It was strange, sitting outside a rented house in Pietersburg, watching the removal men wrap up each item of our furniture. We also bought brand new carpets in Pietersburg for the house in England. We could do that because we had the precise measurements on the sale particulars. The vision – the visualised goal – had become tangible with exact measurements! So the carpets, cut to measure, were wrapped and shipped with the rest of our furniture. And then Jo and our little son Angus left for England with as much of our money as she was allowed. When I followed her in December, I travelled with two friends, each of them having given me a substantial part of their travel allowance. And so I was able to bring over what was left of my capital and I paid off the mortgage on the house!

Our interim objective was accomplished!

It was wonderful, being reunited with my family at the end of 1987. Jo and Angus met me at the railway station in York. She drove me to our house in Harrogate in our very own car – a Rover we had shipped from South Africa. I stepped into the house. Jo had redecorated it with loving care and the new carpets made it feel brand new.

In the spring we went for a walk across the open fields at the back of the house. It was along a public footpath, though you couldn't see the route of the footpath across the overgrown fields. But when you climbed over a turnstile – some neat steps set into a stone wall – you could just make out the next turnstile set into the wall at the other end of a field. And so it went on. Every time we reached a turnstile, we could see the next somewhere in the distance. Sometimes the next one wasn't visible, so we just set out walking in a straight line – and before long we would see it.

Our journey to England had been like that. And it was still to be like that. Now we had got all our assets to England, safely invested in a lovely house, we looked for the next turnstile. It took nearly three months before we could make it out in the distance.

Again, however, this was a period of waiting on the Lord. That is a very important step in goal achievement, for it activates faith – seeing beyond the visible.

STEP SIX

SEEING BEYOND THE VISIBLE
(and waiting on the Lord!)

> To have faith is to be sure of the things
> we hope for, to be certain of the things
> we cannot see.
> *(Hebrews 11:1)*

THE **LORD** tells us that our eyes haven't seen, our ears haven't heard, and that our minds haven't even conceived what he has prepared for us who love him (1 Cor.2:9).

Many say this applies to our future life in the Kingdom of Heaven. Some say it actually applies to this life.

I believe it applies in both cases.

I believe the Lord has prepared a wonderful future for us in this life as well as the next.

By accepting his free gift of eternal life, we have our assurance of salvation in eternity. And the gift of the holy spirit is also our 'earnest' – our first instalment, or promise, our *guarantee* – that we will have eternal life with him in his kingdom (2 Cor. 1:22).

Of course, first we have to *accept* that gift. That's up to us, and requires, once again, an act of initiative – a willingness to receive and an act of acceptance.

And having accepted it, we *belong* to God. We have been purchased with a price. The shed blood of Jesus on the cross was the price. So we no longer have to be punished with death, even though the 'wages of sin is death.' Every man, we're told, has sinned and fallen short of the glory of God. But Jesus, by taking on our punishment for us, has redeemed us. God no longer sees our sin. We are redeemed. We've been purchased with a price, the precious blood of Jesus (1 Cor.6:20).

So we're worth more than many sparrows!

God cares deeply for his redeemed children. We're his heirs. We aren't just useless assets, but jewels in his crown. And because we're precious, he wants to *add* to our glory! Not only in the next life – but in the here and now, or in our imminent future, as we continue to grow in grace.

Jesus has prepared a place for us. He has prepared mansions for us. If we could see beyond the visible, we'd see our mansions.

I said that when Jo and I had reached England, it took three months of waiting on the Lord before we began to discern the next turnstile in our path. It was exciting because it *looked* like a mansion!

It was a *new* objective.

Unlike our compact four-bedroomed house, it had multiple bedrooms and three storeys.

It was either a guest house or a small hotel.

But, as I said, it took a while before we could discern this objective. First, we had to wait on the Lord and seek his guidance. To begin with, I got a temporary job teaching English at a girls' grammar school in Bradford. While engaged in this, I became aware of a vacancy for a youth pastorship at a nearby church. I applied, thinking that was possibly the way the Lord wanted me to feed his lambs! So I applied, and the vicar phoned me and invited me to visit him.

I had to test if this was the Lord's will for me. So on a Friday after school I attempted to find the church. At this point a strange thing happened and certainly helped to test my calling.

My car was hit by a runaway wheel!

I had difficulty in finding the church, so I stopped in the driveway of a garage at the bottom of a steep hill. I got out of the car, and while the garage owner was giving me directions, there was a terrible thud followed by the sound of splintering glass from the other side of the car.

Stunned, I walked around the car. The passenger door had caved in! Glass lay everywhere across the rear seat.

The garage owner picked up a wheel. 'This is what hit you,' he said. But there was no sign of the vehicle from which it had obviously come off. In my shocked condition, I drove on, looking for the offending vehicle. I expected to find it somewhere, crippled, minus a fourth wheel!

But there was nothing.

The calamity didn't end there. I managed temporarily to patch the passenger window with cardboard. The next Monday, when I attempted to reach the Girls' School in the dark of a winter's morning, I couldn't see clearly at an intersection because of the cardboard window! Craning forward and concentrating on the traffic approaching from my left – the blind spot – I was suddenly hit by a car on my right! There was that sickening thud and breaking glass again. At least the poor lady driving the other car was unhurt – as I was. But what a mess! Struck on both sides of the car, my spirit felt broken.

I returned home and wept.

I felt I had lost my way completely.

Here's a poem I wrote at the time. It shows just how depressed and lost I felt. I even felt angry at God. I felt I hadn't been protected when I was following through his command to feed his lambs. I had put my hand to the plough. I had come over to England in faith, and now I began to look back:

Wheel of Destiny

A runaway wheel
hit
my car and collapsed
the door splintering a window in a shower of crushed glass
off the road in Shipley.
I was asking the way to St Peter's to see the vicar
so I thought it a bit thick that God didn't shield me from the blind
clout
of fate furious
that I should dare to seek service as a Youth Pastor.
Sore and bruised by this vicious venom
the next week I tried again to reach Shipley
when in winter dawn dark
I failed to see through the cardboard patched window
and gingerly crept across Wharfdale junction
craning forward to see to the left
when from the right
tearing brakes and rushing lights smashed my tail
spewing glass into my galloping heart
failing for fear as I coasted to safety
knowing I'd rather be dead than suffer consciousness of this loaded
cruelty.
It's that dashed wheel
anonymous with oil in its hub
that skewered loose to skewer my soul that had fled
from anonymous violence in African heat.
Of its mother vehicle there was no sign
yet it seemed a sign to redirect my destiny in a faraway and alien
land

withering my hopes, not nurturing my soul at this crucial
Junction
of my life.
I turned back
from Wharfdale Junction and shall I turn back
to African fury
where no stone nor fire nor wheel
ever necklaced or bruised
my unwilling soul?

*　　*　　*

I received two very comforting letters from two minister friends
to whom I wrote in South Africa. Mike Taylor, a Baptist pastor,
wrote that the wheel incident – what I called the wheel missile! –
would only help me to sharpen my values and to hold *lightly* onto
material things but *tightly* onto eternal things. The accident, he
said, was a means by which we can worship our God for his hand
on us. 'Remember,' he said, 'when things are dark, God does his
greatest work. Think of Calvary: there was darkness for three
hours – and silence reigned! This was when Jesus became sin for
us. What a work! In the darkness of his death the Gospel became
a reality for us!'

The message went home. That accident had taken place in the
bleak darkness of pre-dawn!

'And so,' Mike wrote, 'as you have times of darkness, God is
working, and you – like Jesus – must reaffirm your faith in the
Lord by saying "MY God, MY God," and then be frank with God
and ask him why it seems he has left you.' Mike reminded me
how Jesus, in his darkest hour, had reaffirmed his faith: 'Father,
into your hands I commit my Spirit!' God is faithful. He is near to
receive our all.

'Remember,' Mike concluded, 'the Father seeks worshippers. The
Son seeks sinners. Jesus has saved and found you, now, no matter

what happens. Worship the Father. He is seeking you for that purpose. Worship is doing all for the glory of God.'

I had told my friend Louis Bosch, the Methodist minister, that I thought the wheel missile and the accident were possibly God trying to say something to me. But Louis wrote, 'The accident may not be so much God trying to say something to you as Satan and his wiles attempting to prevent you from doing what you have been led to do in God's Name and for the sake of his Son Jesus!'

Now, however, the answer is clearer. At the intersection I was looking in the wrong direction! And as for the wheel missile – well, time and chance, as Solomon tells us, happens to all of us (Ecc.9:11).

Nevertheless, the incident was a testing device. It was testing my faith. I came out of it with a strengthened faith. I had *grown* a little more – and growing involves growing pains. It also made me look more carefully for my real destiny.

Eventually, I did manage to reach the church and meet the vicar who wanted a youth pastor. He took me round his parish and showed me what my duties would be if I were given the job. I looked at the squash court in one of the church halls, and at the tables for table tennis. 'The job does involve an element of rough and tumble,' the vicar said wryly.

I knew at once this wasn't *me*. Though the job provided opportunities for counselling and evangelism – duties that were close to my heart – it left me cold! I knew at once this wasn't what the Lord wanted me to do. I thought and prayed about it for a week. But my heart remained unmoved. So I withdrew my application. The vicar thanked me for my consideration!

I really don't believe the Lord wants us to serve him in a direction or in a way in which we feel little enthusiasm.

I do believe that, if a direction is right, he will move us *in our hearts and in our spirits!* We are spiritual beings, essentially, and the Lord speaks most closely to us through our own spirits – in our hearts. John, in the Book of Revelation, repeatedly tells us how he was 'carried away in the spirit' when God spoke to him (Rev. 21:10). It is 'the Spirit that bears witness' (1 John 5:6). 'The Spirit itself bears witness with our spirits,' the Apostle Paul says, 'that we are the children of God' (Romans 8:16). The language of the spirit is the language through which the children of God will best understand him.

And so, as my friend the Baptist pastor wrote, 'By applying for the position of youth pastor and then withdrawing, you will have a clearer mind about the Lord's will regarding ministry. Your try was worth it because it was a step to knowing God's guidance and will.'

I didn't go ahead with that application because the Lord hadn't put hooks into my heart!

The whole experience, including the accidents that went with it, helped me to find my way and look more carefully for the Lord's will for me. 'All things work together for good for those that love the Lord.' That's why I've called my poem, retrospectively, 'Wheel of Destiny'! – now the title of one of my published novels.

I looked into my heart. What did I most *want* to do?

That's where I found the next turnstile. Or, to vary the metaphor, I unsealed my heart to find the co-ordinates for my next destination!

It was Jo who helped me to open those sealed orders. She reminded me how we had contemplated the idea of a guest house in Britain – in 1984, when we were in that lovely glen in Scotland. She had been right when, in 1984, she had said, 'I feel this year holds my future.' It was the year when we had discussed the idea of a guest house and found our hearts respond with joy! We had seen it as a means of providing a living while we exercised our gifts of hospitality and developed our skills at writing. At the time, of course, I had acquired my Rolls Royce and then the dream had been forgotten.

Of course, every year holds our future. Every day is a new opportunity to change our future! We are all historians, because every day we're writing – *making* – our own futures! It's futile to speak of how things *might* have been. We can't change our past. Talking about lost opportunities is wasted energy unless we can glean a lesson from our talk. But we *can* do something about tomorrow's today, and tomorrow's past, *today!*

So, as soon as my job at the Girls' School finished at the end of February, we began to look at guest houses for sale. Before we began our quest Jo and I united in prayer, holding hands, and asked the Lord to guide us.

At first we looked at guest houses in the English Lake District. We soon realised the most viable guest house businesses in the Lakes would cost at least twice as much as our house in Harrogate! It was daunting and stretched our faith. We saw one guest house in Keswick. It was set rather away from the tourist traffic in a back street, built of Lakeland stone (which, to my eyes, gave it a dingy appearance). But it had seven letting bedrooms and a very comfortable owner's attached cottage.

Best of all, it was just up the road from the Keswick Convention Centre - the Mecca in England for born-again Christians every July.

What a superb Christian guest house it would make, I thought. But we couldn't possibly afford it. 'Well,' I said, 'let's just take one step at a time.'

So we contacted an estate agent who evaluated our house in Harrogate. Here was a surprise! The agent said he would put it on the market at a price that was nearly twice as much as the price we'd paid for it a year before.

It felt like a miracle! The next step was to make the offer on the guest house subject to the sale of our house in Harrogate. Filled with the wonder of the whole situation, I made the offer. The guest house had been on the market for a year. And yet, when I put in my offer it was only to find that someone else had travelled down from Scotland the day before and bought it!

Pipped at the post! And yet the guest house had been on the market for a whole year!

Well, what had happened? After all, the owners' had seemed quite happy to sell to us, too. And then, I *had* acted in faith. I had asked the Lord for his blessing. I had asked for courage to go ahead. The doors had seemed to be sliding open, miraculously. I was terrified by the notion of taking on a large mortgage, and yet I hadn't backed down. But just when I reached the doors, they slid firmly shut!

Well, we concluded, *that* place wasn't what the Lord had in mind for us. We argued our loss was due to divine intervention! It had been so uncanny, the way it had been whipped away from under our noses. And, after all, the Lord knows what's best for us. We concluded that if it had been the Lord's will for us to have that guest house, nothing would have stopped us getting it provided we showed trust and initiative and courage.

We had taken up our beds and walked!

So at least we felt confident we hadn't failed in our faith.

We took five different trips to the Lake District from Harrogate at the time. It was early spring and we soon realised that prospective buyers were sitting around like vultures, waiting to buy almost any guest house or hotel for sale in the Lake District. It was the last of the Thatcherite years and property prices were booming!

Quite understandably, I suppose, the estate agents used a free-for-all system: instead of a seller accepting a buyer's offer and then waiting for the buyer to sell his own property, he simply sold to the first person who was able to hand over the cash. This meant we could sell our house in Harrogate, only to find in the meantime that the guest house under our offer had been 'gazumped' by another buyer! First come first served! Therefore, the only feasible way to acquire a guest house would be to sell our house first, and *then* look at what's available and buy the one closest to our ideal. Of course, it could mean we would have to settle for second best, or none at all. We could find ourselves homeless and without income if there wasn't anything suitable at the time. It's a system quite different from the one I was used to in South Africa – or in Scotland, for that matter – where an offer, if accepted, is binding on both sides.

Nevertheless, in March, we did find two other guest houses for sale – one in Keswick and one in Windermere. Both were attractive propositions, but in each case, as before, we were 'gazumped' – someone else beat us to the post!

So the doors had slid shut again.

And again, we *had* prayed about each property. We had visualised just how we would redecorate the rooms and where we would fit in our furniture.

Again, we had taken up our beds and were prepared to walk. Or so we believed.

And again, the doors closed just when they seemed to be opening.

But a prayer-request refused is not a prayer unanswered. After all, the Lord, in his wisdom, knows best. He knows what's best for us.

And so I said to Jo, 'We must wait on the Lord.'

Jo said at the time that the future looked gloomy. For one thing, it had become too late in the year to buy a guest house. By the time we found a buyer for our house, and by the time contracts were exchanged, we would have missed the trading season. Then we would hardly be in a position to pay the huge mortgage, especially through the following winter months. And, for another thing, Jo was expecting a new baby in September! As the bank manager in Keswick so kindly pointed out, 'Your timing for buying a business isn't right.'

Perhaps that's why the Lord hadn't opened the doors!

So again I said, 'We'll just have to wait on the Lord.'

But it meant my having to leave Jo and our small son Angus in July and return for a while to South Africa. I hadn't been able to find a permanent or even semi-permanent job in Britain, so had to go back to that Dark Continent where I could at least be sure of a job. Indeed, in resuming my old professorship, I was at least able to send the bulk of my salary to Jo every month.

This is the strategy that we most dreaded – being separated.

In the meantime we had no choice but to hope – and see beyond the visible. It was a good opportunity to clarify our goal.

STEP SEVEN

REACHING OUT

REACHING OUT is the final step that brings your plan together. But it was some time before I had the courage to let go, once again, and to reach out properly – in faith and confidence – towards my goal of a guest house or hotel.

When I returned to South Africa I had not yet let go the old securities. Not altogether, since I resumed my university professorship in South Africa for another year. It's easy to rationalise this move back, of course. It was picking up a lifeline, again, re-establishing an old security because there was a baby on the way. Jo and I wanted to venture, but now our instinct was to nest. So we provided a secure nest for the baby while I went away, back to a salary far away.

But it was hanging on tenaciously to a job for which I had no more real commitment. My heart wasn't in it. It was a miserable year. Twice I flew back to England, during university vacations. I was commuting across the world. And it was miserable! A life of separation from one's spouse and family is not a life to be recommended. It was a life in the wilderness, a life of agony. 'That's very hard!' was the heartfelt response of my fellow passenger on the aeroplane when I told him I was leaving my family in England to work abroad. He was an academic and a Christian, like me – but he was surrounded by his wife and two lively sons.

Once, before I had returned to South Africa, I was speaking to the managing director of a large company. He was surprised when I told him I was returning temporarily to my job in South Africa. Staying on in South Africa for the sake of sending the pitiful sum of £500 a month to my wife was ridiculous, he said. Even his teenage son, he told me, could earn that amount – helping out in a baker's shop! My idea, I said, was to hold on to a secure salary while Jo started up a business. He laughed: 'It would be better to be with her, if only to push a broom! A business doesn't run itself! It doesn't run on remote control. To succeed, it demands total involvement and total personal commitment.'

But I wanted to play it safe. I wanted a lifeline while Jo had the baby, sold the house, found a suitable guest house or hotel, *and* established the business! Poor Jo! And, at best, my salary was a tenacious lifeline – a lifeline that was more like an umbilical cord.

When my father died in April 1989 it was easier for me to cut the cord. The new baby had arrived safely, too, and Jo got a job as a receptionist in a large hotel in Harrogate – which, of course, was good preparation for our goal apart from providing a salary. So there was nothing, really, to hold me in South Africa. Jo had to employ a nanny to look after the baby, and my professorial salary, ravaged by the now outrageous exchange rate, barely paid the nanny's wages! So, at worst, I could save just as much by taking on the job of nanny to my own baby son!

So, finally, I let go – again! I resigned my job. I recall the amazement of one of the university secretaries who came up to my table in the canteen. 'A senior professor doesn't just resign!' she exclaimed. My students (all of them African) invited me to a farewell function in the Great Hall. There were five hundred of them. I was touched as they spoke of the 'great man' leaving them. I pointed out that the only way I could lay claim to greatness was by the size of my paunch. I gave them a little speech of my own, telling them not to be afraid to venture, to face change in a country that needed change. Much of this exhortation was to reinforce my own resolve to face change. I quoted Robert Frost's poem 'The Road Not Taken'. Again, I was at the cross-roads, a junction in the road of life, and I had to make a choice. This time I was going to take that road not taken by the vast majority of commuters and the army of secure salaried personnel.

An adventure, I'm told, is a journey with an unpredictable outcome, or uncertain finish. It's this mystery or unpredictability that gives it the dimension of fun, no doubt. The element of risk produces a *frisson* of excitement.

True. But a successful undertaking must also have a clearly visualised goal, or objective. In a sense, success is a result of both – a marriage between risk and a strategy of careful planning. There is daring, on the one hand, and there is a clear objective, on the other. The risk is the walking on water, and the reaching out while on the water. Planning minimises the risk. Faith, in the end, eliminates it.

Having resigned my job permanently, this time, there was no more looking back. I had burned my last bridge. Now I found myself confronted by a whole new ball game! Until now I had always bought myself a return ticket to South Africa, valid for one year. Now, for the first time, I bought a one-way ticket to the United Kingdom! It felt good, as I waited for my flight at the airport. I was going home! Home was no longer in the past. Home was where I was going, in the imminent future! I was reminded of the Lord's advice: 'He who places his hand on the plough and looks back is not worthy of the Kingdom of God.' Life is certainly a practical training ground for the Kingdom!

And what joy awaited me on my return to Jo! She met me at King's Cross station, where I saw the bundle of my new son for the first time. He was more interested in his next feed than seeing his father! Then we made our way to Lunar House in Croyden where the next joyful event awaited me. I had applied to have my residence in the United Kingdom extended, and it was normal to expect no more than a year's extension at a time. After a long wait in queues, and a number of bottle feeds, my passport was returned with a new document. I looked at it with unbelief. I had become a *permanent* resident of the United Kingdom! Quite unexpectedly, another door had opened.

But another phase of waiting was in store. It was only six months, but it felt like years, before we had an offer on our house in Harrogate. Indeed, we came close to being deflected from our planned goal of a guest house or hotel. I was about to sign an agreement to enter an 'Art Shop' franchise. But on the morning of the very day I planned to sign the agreement and send my deposit for a thousand pounds, the phone rang. It was my garage mechanic. 'I believe your house is on the market?' he said. That evening he brought his wife around and, in the end, bought the house.

In any case, little Bruce must have benefited from the intensive interaction with his father-nanny. We played together and I became quite adept at changing nappies. Jo had unsociable hours, working as a hotel receptionist, and it was always a joy to hear her car pull up shortly after midnight.

While we waited for the exchange of contracts we resumed our search for a guest house or small hotel. We combed through many sale particulars. It was exciting, now, to identify our goal in terms of bricks and mortar, in terms of real geographical location and business viability. It was the excitement of seeing for the first time our objective – our visualised ideal in real life. It was like the first time I saw my Rolls Royce – a Polaroid picture sent through the post from a dealer in London, back in 1984. This time it was a picture on the sale particulars sent by an estate agent in Scotland.

'*That's* it!' I pronounced, as soon as my eyes fell on it. It was a Victorian villa in stone, in two stories, dormer windows on top. From that moment the goal possessed me. It matched up with the picture in my mind. I knew it existed somewhere – I just had to find it! Best of all, because our house in Harrogate had increased in value, the Kenmore Bank Hotel in Jedburgh was in our price range!

It was in 1984, our year in Scotland, and the year which Jo felt held our future, that we first conceived the idea of a guest house or hotel and found our hearts responding with joy: so it's not surprising, perhaps, that we should have discovered our hotel in Scotland! All those trips to the Lake District weren't futile, of course. They were a limbering up in the search for our ultimate ideal. As someone said, Scotland is a much bigger lake district!

The legal machinery rolled slowly but surely. But our offer on the hotel was accepted and, on the first day of March 1990, in the middle of a snowstorm, we moved into our hotel. It was just right for us, with private bedrooms and a private sitting room for the family. From the sloping lawn of the front garden, the elegant dining room and upper levels, we enjoyed sweeping, open views of Jedburgh Abbey, the Jed Water that flowed just below us, and the ancient town of Jedburgh. Angus and Bruce (their names show how unconsciously or consciously we had been aiming for Scotland!) had a private yard and ample scope to grow. In the summer seasons of the first few years Angus wore his kilt regularly to serve our guests in the dining room. The guests loved him: by the end of the first season he had earned enough money in tips to buy his own computer!

And we loved our guests. We were thrilled to meet so many gracious and complimentary people, from Scotland, England, the Continent, Australia, Canada and America.

Surely the wait, even the interlude in the wilderness of frustration and separation from the family, was worth it in the end. There are lessons to learn, of course, from this exercise in change. One lesson is the value of perseverance, of the tenacity of hope. It's not an easy ride, letting go of a secure income as one approaches fifty. I had to let go to grow, but not let go of hope. And, indeed, I'm regularly reminded that the most essential quality for survival, in any situation involving change, is a positive attitude. It's vital when circumstances alter, when new circumstances test one, pushing one beyond the point ever gone before. One's worst enemies are complacency, just sitting back, letting things happen, putting up with a bad lot, or holding back, even giving up, out of fear or a negative attitude. In her book *Mind Magic* Betty Shine speaks of the energy-producing power of a positive mind, and warns of the destructive, undermining energy of a negative mind. In some strange way a positive mind actually releases energy, to heal both body and mind, enabling one to survive the journey of change towards the new lifestyle that it pre-empts.

How often I had thought, in that struggling time in Harrogate, of shipping all my belongings, and my money, back to the country I had left! How comfortable it would have been to take advantage of the horrendous exchange rate, for going back it would be in my favour. I could have been a millionaire in rands!

But I was often reminded of our Lord's words – he who puts his hands to the plough, and looks back, is unworthy of the divine Kingdom. And I had glanced back so often – just like the Israelites, longing for the flesh pots of Egypt in their journey through the wilderness. It's only human to look back. There were times when I thought of what I had given up – my comfortable suburban home, my swimming pool, my three cars including my Rolls; also, my caravan, my steady income, my pension. How unworthy I am of the Kingdom! And yet, this grand exercise in change, like life itself, is a training programme, no doubt for the Kingdom of God.

Certainly change, like significant growth, is not easy. It was never meant to be. It's interesting how often my guests asked me: 'But why did you do it? Why did you leave your academic career?' (Many of my academic guests would say: 'I wish *I* had done it!" One heartfelt observation came from a professor, an ex-colleague in South Africa: 'Charles, I envy you!') But in asking me the question 'why?', they certainly put their fingers on a burning question. 'I don't know,' I replied, at times: 'Because I hated marking papers and attending faculty meetings!' If I were feeling properly positive, I would say, 'Because it's what I *wanted*. It's what I aimed for.' But in those early months I often replied, truthfully, 'I don't know!' In the first months I often lay awake, asking myself the question. There were moments when I thought I was mad to do it!

Change from a secure routine will invoke these sleepless nights, at first. These moments of panic can recur unexpectedly, unless they are countered by a sustained positive attitude! And a positive attitude, as Norman Vincent Peale has revealed in his works on positive thinking, is engendered by a *disciplined programming* of the mind with positive thoughts. Daily meditation on the following faith-engendering passages from the Bible, for instance, will release a powerful flow of healing energy:

*   *   *

To have faith is to be sure of the things we hope for, to be certain of the things we cannot see.
(Heb. 11:1)

No one can please God without faith, for whoever comes to God must have faith that God exists and rewards those who seek him.
(Heb. 11:6)

We know that in all things God works for good with those who love him, those whom he has called according to his purpose.
(Romans 8:28)

Be joyful always, pray at all times, be thankful in all circumstances. This is what God wants from you in your life in union with Christ Jesus.
(1 Thess.5:16)

I assure you that if you believe and do not doubt, you will be able ... to say to this hill, 'Get up and throw yourself in the sea,' and it will. If you believe, you will receive whatever you ask for in prayer.
(Matt. 21:21-22)

May the God of peace provide you with every good thing you need in order to do his will, and may he, through Jesus Christ, do in us what pleases him.
(Heb. 13:21)

... if any of you lacks wisdom, he should pray to God, who will give it to him ... But when you pray, you must believe and not doubt at all.
(James 1: 5-6)

I keep striving to win the prize for which Christ Jesus has already won me to himself ...; the one thing I do ... is to forget what is behind me and do my best to reach what is ahead.
(Phil. 12-13)

His angel guards those who honour the Lord and rescues them from danger. ... those who obey him have all they need.
(Psalm 34:7-9)

I have the strength to face all conditions by the power that Christ gives me.
(Philip. 4:3)

... those who trust in the Lord for help
will find their strength renewed.
They will rise on wings like eagles;
they will run and not get weary;
they will walk and not grow weak.
(Isaiah 40:31)

If you remain in me and my words remain in you, then you will ask for anything you wish, and you shall have it.
(John 15:7)

... be concerned above everything else with the Kingdom of God and with what he requires of you, and he will provide you with all these other things. So do not worry about tomorrow...
(Matt. 6:33-34)

Ask, and you will receive; seek, and you will find; knock, and the door will be opened to you...
(Matt. 7:7)

*   *   *

Setting aside a 'quiet time' daily, early in the morning and also in the evening, to meditate on passages such as these, produces an effervescence of faith, of energy that heals the mind and makes one courageous to dare – to stretch out and grasp the opportunities at hand. The released energy turns one's eyes away from the past, or the turmoil in the present, or the anxieties of daily life. It recharges the mind and the failing heart, and turns one's face to the source of power. Faith is forward-looking – forward-working energy – like the faith of Peter walking on the water, keeping his eyes off the seething waves, fixed on Jesus, his hands reaching out for the strength of his arm.

Having achieved my objective – my hotel in Scotland – my next concern was to ensure my business was *viable*. Releasing the energy of faith, looking forward as I entered my first trading season, I was able to activate two positive principles of enterprise. I shall endow these with a 'one way' sign (to borrow a symbol from the *Highway Code*), because they are positive, mandatory instructions:

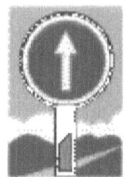

1. Plan ahead

2. Think customer

Planning ahead is reaching out in advance. *Thinking customer* is essential if you want your product to be sold to your targeted market sector.

I soon realised my market sector was largely what is known as 'Empty nest, phase one and two' – in other words, people in their fifties or sixties, whose children have already left home, and the recently retired. Imagining myself in their place, I appreciated their need for warm hospitality and comfortable, *en suite* facilities. Not many of my bedrooms were equipped with private facilities – private toilets, showers or baths. During the season we kept a careful record of the number of times we lost the sale of a bedroom because it had no bath or shower of its own. By the end of the season we estimated that our occupancy rate could be improved by at least 25% if private facilities were installed throughout.

Here was an area of obvious growth. We had an architect draw up the necessary plans. By the end of the season the planning permission and building control consents had been obtained, and work began in November. We might have received a generous grant from the Scottish Tourist Board if I'd been patient, but I was anxious to begin the alterations before the worst of the winter weather set in. Indeed, large sections of the roof had to be removed and rebuilt. Two large dormer extensions were constructed to the rear, to house the shower and toilet facilities in the attic bedrooms. This dramatically changed the appearance and the practical value of the top bedrooms: they appeared larger, the ceilings had been raised, but most important, my guests occupying these rooms would no longer need to trek downstairs in the middle of the night to reach a bathroom!

For nearly three months the building shook and shuddered as builders broke through walls and swarmed over the roof with hammers, saws and drills. Jo and I worked through long nights repapering and repainting. And in the end we had a dramatically changed and upgraded building, each bedroom gift-wrapped in co-ordinating wallpaper, border friezes, plush carpets and bedding. When the army of joiners, plumbers, plasterers and electricians eventually left, Jo and I wandered from bedroom to bedroom, admiring the finished product. When a party of Welsh choristers returned at the end of January, many found themselves in the same rooms they had occupied before. They took turns inspecting one-another's rooms, marvelling at the transformation.

'Look, I've got my own shower!'

'Come and see. My bathroom has gold taps and marble walls!'

It was fun watching for their reaction. 'You have a lovely home,' the leader of the party said at the end of their stay.

We felt it had been worth it. The business was more viable, now. But – were we going to afford all the costs? The tradesmen's bills, and the architect's bill (he had made countless journeys from Edinburgh, and drawn up so many plans), were yet to come in. And we knew the total cost would be much, much higher than the original estimates.

Getting quotations at the outset was part of the advance planning, of course. But it's amazing how quotations are knocked to pieces by unexpected plumbing problems and electrical difficulties. Our building was mid-Victorian, and the plumbers and electricians found that much more work was involved than originally anticipated in the complex re-routing of pipes and cables. Also, the complicated engineering required by the Building Control authorities in the construction of the dormers escalated the scale of work dramatically. And because the alterations went through Christmas and New Year, we lost all the trade that the festive season might have brought.

This brings me to the other two important principles vital for business success. I've marked these with a 'no entry' sign because they are warning, or prohibitory, instructions:

3. Don't run out of cash!

4. Don't expand too quickly.

Cashflow is the lifeblood of any business. If it ceases, or dries up, the business dies.

The spectre of running out of cash, now that we had potentially improved the business, was one which haunted us until the new flow of visitors in the spring. We had calculated that we had enough cash to weather the winter season *and* do the alterations – in the extra amount added to the mortgage when we bought the business, and by the savings put aside during the season. But the much higher costs, the deepening recession, the high interest rates *and* the Gulf War, were factors we hadn't allowed for. Had we, therefore, expanded too quickly? We hadn't fallen into the trap of acquiring an expensive, prestigious car, to make the business look good, or improve the comfort of our private living quarters; we *had* ploughed all the money we had earned – and more – back into the business. But should we nevertheless have waited another season? The opportunity, the hard evidence for successful growth, had been too strong to resist. So we had reached out.

Again, it's the sustained positive attitude that kept us going, looking forward, not backwards. The time was right, we had felt, to take the opportunity so close to our grasp. As Shakespeare says,

> There is a tide in the affairs of men,
> Which, taken at the flood, leads on to fortune.
> *(Julius Caesar*, IV. iii).

Besides, we so much *wanted* to grow, and *wanted* to keep trading as a hotel. It's a job we found we liked and it brought joy into our lives through the people we met. There's something about loving and enjoying your work that engenders success. Most people, the army of commuters and wage-earners, don't enjoy their work. It's something they *have* to do. One's attitude towards money, however, determines one's success. As I said in Step Two of this guide, progress is fired by enthusiasm, or real desire. It's the steam that drives the engine. Money, like bread, will come back to you if you cast it on the waters – with love and confidence. In a spirit of prayerful seeking, we must look into our own heart's desire – and there we may well find God's will for us. As I said before, the Lord so often puts hooks into our hearts. In other words, we must *want* to do something, and to enjoy doing it, before the Lord will bless the endeavour. In this sense I believe the Lord is willing to be our Spiritual – and Senior – partner in business. The venture must bear his stamp of approval and blessing of joy. And then, if he is *for* us, who can be against us?

Jo and I, despite our new financial hurdle, were facing our second season with joy and hope. We couldn't wait to bestow our improved gift of hospitality on our guests! We faced the new season not with fear or trepidation, but with joyful anticipation. 'Do you *want* to walk?' Jesus had asked the paralysed man. 'Yes,' the man replied – and he took up his bed and walked!

To release his power and strength to us, Jesus requires us to reach out, positively, not just with our hearts, but with our wills. In a sense, I suppose, Jo and I willed the success of our business. We reached out – into an active marketing programme. We didn't wait for the angel to stir the waters. So far as we could plan forward and take the initiative, we did: we had postcards printed with a bright picture of the hotel (reproduced from an oil painting); we advertised the hotel in many of the local Scottish Tourist Board guides, including colour photographs; and we advertised in golfing magazines, for the Scottish Borders are blessed with many scenic and uncrowded fairways. (A package deal including accommodation and green fees was to become one of our most successful ventures: in our third season; golfers accounted for at least one third of our turnover!) But the greatest reason for our success is something we can't account for – in precise or scientific terms! Ultimately, it was a step-by-step dependence on the Lord's daily supply, especially in those early days when debts still hung over us. This mystery of God's supply, of his ever-loving care, is something I have tried to explain in the epilogue. One thing I do know: it is an outcome of simple, unwavering faith.

Look again at the faith passages I listed. Through faith strength is won out of weakness. If we have undoubting faith, and ask for the removal of the mountain (financial hurdle or other obstacle to success), 'it will be done.' A positive faith or attitude activates divine power. It releases the power within us, like yeast – God's will 'working in me'; and by being a 'doer, not a hearer only', we shall be blessed in our doing. A positive attitude leads to positive action, which activates the positive energy from God. There is a supply line ready to channel energy to us: God's power station operates on a self-service basis – it's not enough to pull up and hoot and expect a uniformed angel to rush out and top us up! We have to recognise our Source, reach out and grasp the billion-star energy line.

It's a wonderful thought, that God who has placed the stars in the universe interrelates with and provides energy for each and every one of us. It's a power more vast than we can comprehend. Not only prayer (praise and asking), but action releases this power. And with this release cones peace and joy. This lesson of joy and power in God –directed change – is encapsulated in some apt phrases from that marvellous hymn *All my hope on God is founded:*

Me through change and chance he guideth...
He calls my heart to be his own...
But God's power is my temple and my tower...
His desire our soul delighteth...
Joy doth wait on his command...
Ye who follow shall not fall.

Dramatic change in lifestyle will certainly result in sleepless nights. The antidote is to focus the heart and mind, in praise and prayer, knowing that tomorrow's action will release the power to conquer! Tomorrow, as we walk and grow upwards, we'll be supplied with new strength. How reassuring to know that as we reach out, step out and 'march on', we'll 'never grow faint!' Our growth will be visible *upwards* as we use our Eagles' wings.

Visible growth, of course, is always upwards. It is *phototropic* – growing towards the light. God may live in light unapproachable by man – but our strength is enhanced as we grow towards his light. Without his light our growth will cease and we shall wither.

But growth is also *geotropic* and *hydrotropic,* botanists tell us. A plant must send its roots downwards, into the earth. It must be anchored in a firm foundation from which it will also take its water and nutrition. So our visible growth upwards is preceded by subterranean growth – conceiving our goal, planning ahead, working out a strategy; and, sooner than we may expect, we will break through, sending shoots downwards as we lift our heads upwards, resolutely reaching out for our goal. Breaking through, in business terms, is breaking even, establishing viability and solid security. This is not achieved overnight. Growth is gradual, but it's sure, and before long will be in reach of the planned objective.

As I look back now, it took us *seven years* – seven years to effect the transition from a suburban housewife and university professor in South Africa to the owner-proprietors of a financially viable hotel in Scotland. Since then we purchased and sold two houses, paid off the mortgage on the hotel in full, and went on a world cruise with our two sons.

Had we been bolder, more daring, more trusting, perhaps, we might have achieved our goal in less time. But we had to overcome a collapsing economy in South Africa and currency restrictions designed to prevent emigration. But, at least, we persevered. And we grew stronger in the process. We had learnt to overcome obstacles, to become spiritual opportunists and entrepreneurs, stepping out towards closed doors, finding the ones that God, in his divine plan and wisdom, was willing to open for us.

Most important, it proved to be a transition from routine complacency, from commuter boredom, from political unease, to real job satisfaction and joyful fulfilment.

The first sense of real joy hit home when I walked into the Church of Scotland in Jedburgh. There, below the high Victorian pulpit, was a wooden structure, like a smaller pulpit in wood. From my position in the congregation it looked like a writing desk.

Surely I'd seen it before! It was so like the one I described at the end of Step Four of this guide ('Tapping into the spirit dimension'). My heart missed a beat when I saw it. I had been half expecting to see it, somewhere – and I knew that surely I was on course, that I was where God wanted me to be. I knew, at least, that despite all the lost opportunities, his hand was here, guiding me. Indeed, I knew then that he had never left me. (Later I asked the minister about the wooden structure. He called it a prayer box. Whenever he prayed during the service, he entered it.)

Perhaps I shouldn't have been surprised when, just a few weeks later, the minister of the same church phoned me. Would I take the morning service while he was away on holiday? *Would I!*

The Sunday on which I took the morning service was Father's Day. That took my thoughts back to my own father, who had died just over a year before. I told the congregation how, in his last months, he had cut out a great many little hearts from cardboard; on each he had stuck a little spray of dried flowers and carefully written a biblical verse. Each heart had a different verse. He had intended these little hearts to be handed out to all the mothers on Mothers' Day Sunday at the Methodist Church he belonged to in South Africa. But he died before Mothers' Day. I found the shoe box he kept, filled to the brim with these bright hearts, and duly gave them all to my friend Louis, the minister of my father's church. And Louis handed the hearts to the mothers after the service. I hadn't kept any of the hearts back, and asked for one as I left the church. It was my way of looking for a special message from my heavenly Father. I looked at the heart I had lifted out of the bag. I admit to some disappointment when I read, in my dad's copperplate writing: 'You are all I want, O Lord' (Psalm 119: 57).

Perhaps I was hoping for one of those faith passages I listed earlier; or a passage that promised me anything I wanted, as in Mark 11:24: 'Whatever you ask in prayer, believe that you receive it and it shall be yours.' That passage always meant a great deal to me. I recall reading how Norman Vincent Peale used it as a basis for thanking the Lord in advance for a gift or blessing, before it was received, as an act of faith. It was the kind of reinforcement to my faith I was looking for. It's a passage, perhaps, that appealed to my materialistic instinct.

Instead, I was told, the Lord was sufficient – he was *all* I should want!

And therein, of course – *of course!* – lies the total answer to our quest. Using that verse as the text for my sermon made me realise God himself is what anybody and everybody ultimately wants – and needs. Anything less will never satisfy. Did my Rolls Royce satisfy me? Did my professorship, my university degrees and doctorates, satisfy me? Would my hotel be my *raison d'être*? No! God was – *is* – the answer.

'Seek ye *first* the Kingdom of God, and all these things shall be added unto thee.'

We can be sure that when we have committed ourselves to God, we have placed ourselves in the hands of a loving Father. We are heirs to his kingdom, and it's our Father's loving will for us that we receive his inheritance. 'In my Father's house are many mansions.' Jesus has assured us of our place in God's scheme of things.

When we've committed ourselves to God – through accepting his only Son – we're assured of a place in his kingdom. We're assured of the high privilege of Jesus forever abiding with us: and through Jesus, we abide with God.

'You are all I want, O Lord.' That's the Father's greatest desire for us – himself.

It's the first commandment – to love God with all our heart, our mind, with all our soul. To live, and move, and have our being in God, is his greatest desire for us. We are his heart's desire, and if we are his, he places the same desire for him in *our* hearts.

And, I believe, the whole of life is a preparation for this eternal abiding with the Father. To this end the ways of providence are meant to lead us. 'All things work together for good for those who love him.' God made us for himself – for his eternal pleasure.

When we fall in love, we surrender our hearts to someone. When we recognise our calling from God and accept him, we are yielding to God who is Love – and the greatest power source in the universe. Our utilisation of this power will be in proportion to the extent we have surrendered to him. From the day we accept Jesus as our saviour, we accept the father's love. His Providence, his Power, will uphold us, sustain and also mould us. All you – and I – can do is let his power and love take over.

Of course we can have anything we really want! In accepting the only begotten Son of God, we have become heirs of the Father – joint heirs with his son Jesus. All that is his, is yours, and mine. Eye has not seen, nor ear heard, nor has it entered into our hearts, what he has prepared for us – we who love him. He wants to bless us beyond all measure, precisely because we are his sons and daughters. But before he can bless us in full measure, before we can come into our divine inheritance, he will change us. Change is good for us – and he will certainly change us in accordance with his divine plan and purpose.

In seeking change, in reaching out towards a goal – even if it's a small, interim goal in our lives – we are, consciously or unconsciously, becoming part of a divine plan and purpose. Change, after all, is growth.

Our growth will be expedited if we reach out to God, and identify our goal as part of his plan for us. If we reach out for God, we will know he has already reached out for us: we will find ourselves in his hands! And the wonderful news is that, once we're in the hands of the living God, he will *never let us go!* His word is a lamp to our path, and we have his assurance that he will direct our ways. We need to discern his will for us – examine our gifts, abide in him, and grow in him, until we can truly say, 'You are all I want, O Lord!'

The author's hotel in Scotland – from a painting by his youngest daughter, Carol Bathgate

Epilogue

IT'S CERTAINLY TRUE. You *can* have anything you *really* want. You must identify it as a clear goal, and visualise it clearly. You must really want it, with all your heart. This releases your own energy, or motivation. You must then work out a strategy, a progressive plan, with steps, or deadlines. You must engender patience, and perseverance. Most important of all, you must reach out, in faith and confidence.

This reaching out in faith takes place not only at the end, but at the beginning of the programme.

It's the reaching out in faith that releases an energy *outside* yourself.

This energy will not only realise your goal, but will change you in the reaching out. You may find that it changes the goal you desire, because it may have changed you inwardly.

When I reached out in faith and attained my Rolls Royce, I found I had been changed in the process.

The same applies to my university degrees. I attained all the degrees I set out to attain. By the time my study wall was loaded with framed certificates, I found I had been changed.

The same applied to my professorship, which I held for ten years.

It was like the time I wanted to fly, when I was in my late teens. As soon as I had my pilot's licence, after the thrill of those first solo flights in a Cessna 150 were over, the desire to continue flying left me.

I had been changed.

Reaching out in faith changes one. It changes your goals.

That's the risk you take, when you accept God as your partner in the enterprise. And it's God who does the changing! After each achievement, one seeks a worthier goal. If you ask God to be your Senior partner in business, he will change you, mature you, and make you grow into a less materialistic person. So beware! You may end up wanting God, just for himself. If you do, praise the Lord, for his goal involves a perfect plan for you – one which he conceived even before you were born.

I enlisted God in the seeking and realisation of all my goals. In his mercy and love, he allowed me to achieve them. After all, they were deeply rooted in my heart – in my desire. It was good for me to achieve them, and therefore part of his plan for me that I should realise them. But sometimes he helps you – or allows you – to achieve a goal so you can experience the emptiness of that goal. Then he will substitute that goal for a new goal – one which will glorify and serve him! After all, that's why he created us in the first place.

Once, when I was half asleep early one morning, the words formed in my mind: *'I am your Senior Partner in the Garden of Life.'* That was back in South Africa, before I sold my house there and decided to leave. The impression of the words was very strong, so I got up and wrote them down: 'I am your Senior Partner in the Garden of Life.'

It was a strange concept, I remember thinking, because it expressed a mixed metaphor. It said God was my partner – my senior partner – which suggested a business relationship – one in which he had the authority to dictate terms and veto decisions, to initiate enterprises and strategies, and to take control as well as responsibility. But the business was the 'Garden of Life' – a concept suggesting a living, organic, changing, growing force. In a garden there is also beauty and order. As a gardener God also plans and prunes, so that the garden will glorify its maker. Our praise for God, and our trust in him, and our acceptance of his will and his plan for us as he prunes away our selfishness and self-reliance, and as he feeds and waters us, will reflect greater glory on him.

In the process, of course, we are being changed, constantly. We are partners, but we're also part of the Garden.

As business partners we have the right to approach our Senior Partner and ask for whatever we need. Paul wrote, 'In union with Christ and through our faith in him we have the boldness to go into God's presence with all confidence' (Eph.3:12). Jesus himself told his followers that anyone *believing* in him would be able to perform miracles, and could approach the Father: 'I will do whatever you ask for in my name, so that the Father's glory will be shown through the Son' (John 14: 13).

As business partners we have the right to ask without a whining, self-effacing humility. We can have a positive image of ourselves in so far as we bear the image of Christ himself – and in so far as God has made us in his image. We have a more than adequate self-image, since we are covered by the love of Christ. If we are redeemed by his blood, he has paid the price of our sins, so we can approach God fearlessly, without cringing, and without false-humility.

And so, in 'all your prayers ask God for what you need' (Phil.4:6). Our Senior Partner doesn't expect us to beg. We come to him, rather, as a business partner to the senior partner, or to the owner himself, bringing cheques or invoices to be signed, knowing that to lay the matter before him means immediate supply.

Merlin Carothers, in his books *Prison to Praise* and *Power in Praise,* has explained how our acceptance of every little thing that happens to us, with joy and thanksgiving, will release the power of God in and through us. When we set out to achieve anything and reach out for a goal, we need to accept, first, that we are precisely where God wants us to be at that moment. In asking God for anything, we need to thank him first for every little detail of our lives, for all those details and circumstances are used by God in working out his special plan for us. Our praise and thanks, even for apparently adverse circumstances, release his power to work in our lives – either to transform our circumstances, or to transform us. And, as I said, very often we ourselves will be transformed by the transformation of our circumstances!

Perhaps it's not easy for you to accept that God right now has you exactly where he wants you? Can you accept that he hasn't overlooked any little detail?

I've often said, 'Oh, if only I could go back to 1966 – I wouldn't have wasted time studying for university degrees that aren't any use to me now!' Or, 'If only I'd emigrated from South Africa in 1983, just before the collapse of the South African currency – I could have bought a hotel in Scotland outright!' Or, 'If only I hadn't bought the Rolls Royce in 1984: I should have bought a parcel of land in Scotland instead!'

The first thing to do is kick the 'If only' habit! I was delighted when Carothers, in *Power in Praise,* asked if I thought God was helpless to interfere back when I made what I thought of as a wrong choice. What a difference it made when I understood that all things work together for good for those who love the Lord, according to his purpose for them! (Rom.8:28). God has promised us that he makes all things, including our wrong choices, work out for good when we trust him and praise him. God surely allowed my difficult circumstances and possible wrong choices because he knew they were good for me!

I can praise and thank God that I made those seemingly wrong choices. In fact, I can accept that he was willing for me to miss the chance of emigrating in 1983, because it presented me with greater hurdles to overcome. I was given the opportunity to grow up more, to mature spiritually, to develop more trust in him by relying more on his strength. *Of course* he wanted me to have the Rolls Royce, just like we want our children to have a long-cherished toy. He wanted me to have it so I could take my measure of pleasure from it; but also, he wanted me to muster the strength and will to give it up – like giving up a toy, putting away childish things in favour of a greater, more spiritual goal. And he was willing to have me move countries after the collapse of the rand, so I could depend more on his miraculous power to establish me in Scotland – or elsewhere in the world.

The result has been a change within me, a result of a steady process of self-reduction. Of course, I used to take great pride in my personal achievements and in my outward trappings of success. My degrees, my big house, my swimming pool, my Rolls, my published textbooks, my professorship! I remember how it used to rile me, after I was awarded my first doctorate from London University, when I was 28, and people failed to address me by my new title 'Dr'! And later I took great pleasure in being addressed as 'Professor.' And how I enjoyed being saluted by the police in Scotland when I drove my Rolls!

Well, that's all gone now, thanks to the circumstances the Lord led me into.

A rose bush must be pruned to bear perfect roses. Jesus said, 'I am the real vine, and my Father is the gardener. He breaks off every branch in me that does not bear fruit, and he prunes every branch that does bear fruit, so that it will be clean and bear more fruit' (John 15:1-2).

In the Garden of Life all circumstances are in the Gardener's hands!

I remember how Joan, a member of the Baptist Church in Pietersburg to which I once belonged, was involved in an awful head-on collision. She took pride in her wealth and her talent as an accomplished artist. She was driving to her country home in the mountains when an oncoming car careered round a bend, out of control. It hit her head-on. Her next memory was waking up in hospital. That's where I saw her, in the intensive care unit, hooked up to life-support equipment. She barely recognised me. I don't remember how many of her bones were broken. One leg was badly fractured in three places and the doctors thought it would have to be amputated. Much later she told us how she lay there, barely alive, half wanting to die, and praised the Lord. When she was told her leg would have to come off, she was unhappy, but still praised the Lord. When a new set of X-rays were taken the doctors were surprised at the rate of healing, and her heart rejoiced when they told her they weren't going to amputate, after all! And she praised the Lord. When she was released from hospital she walked to the front of the church, unaided, and gave this testimony. She told us how she had been walking in her garden, looking at her rose bushes, praying to the Lord. She told us how his loving words came to her, then: 'I have pruned you, because I love you.' And she praised the Lord.

Praise and thanksgiving release his power to heal and to change. Joan had been healed, and changed too. Her love of God, her calm acceptance of her misfortune and unabated praise to God, was a grand testimony for others, that all things work together for good for those who love the Lord. She had learnt to comfort others, having been comforted and healed herself. (2 Cor.1:5: 'Just as we have a share in Christ's many sufferings, so also through Christ we share in God's great help.')

In a sense, Joan had suffered a reduction of self. Through it, God was glorified.

Self-reduction is one of the prerequisites for self-fulfilment in God's scheme of things. An unwavering faith, or trust, in God, is only possible if our own personal pride and trust in self is expunged. That wonderful outpouring of God's love, the baptism in the Holy Spirit, is designed to help us in this reduction of self, in the total surrender of self to God.

That's what happened at the end of 1984, in that little room in London, when suddenly, without warning, the flood of God's spirit overwhelmed me. As I said earlier, it was like a waterfall of love and light, and my soul wept in total surrender and joy. The abundance of God's love and presence was there, assuring me that I didn't have to apologise or do a thing to earn his love. I went into the morning completely expunged of self, with an overwhelming sense of love for everybody around me.

As Merlin Carothers explains, the baptism of the Holy Spirit is designed to *reduce* us, so that more of God's presence and power can dwell in us and flow through us. Paul praised God who 'by means of his power working in us is able to do so much more than we can ever ask for, or even think of' (Eph.3:20).

So, the Lord will more than answer our prayers, and fulfil us beyond our wildest dreams, and supply us with more than we seek. Our cup will run over beyond all measure, if we surrender self to him. If we have God, we have everything, for 'In him dwelleth all the fullness of the Godhead'; in the words of F.E. Marsh:

> There is in Christ for you
> Fullness of acceptance
> Fullness of peace
> Fullness of life
> Fullness of blessing
> Fullness of power
> Fullness of grace
> Fullness of love
> Fullness of teaching
> Fullness of joy
> Fullness of riches
> Fullness of strength and

Fullness of light;
Therefore, walk with Him.

And in the words of John Newton's hymn, *'The Lord is our power, the Lord will provide.'*

We can be certain God will meet our every need, even if we ask him for something against his will for us. We can trust him absolutely, for, as Jesus said, surely, like a good father, he knows what to give his children. 'Do you suppose a father will give his child a snake or scorpion if he asks for bread? Surely God knows how to give us what we need, far better than an earthly father.' Once even the great prophet Elijah asked for something against God's will. He was feeling terribly dejected. He turned his face to the wall and said, 'It is enough: now, O Lord, take away my life' (1 Kings 19:4). I confess I have felt like that, even after my spirit baptism, and after I had made the journey of faith to Scotland. It was in the early days of owning the hotel. The expenses were running up and trade was slow to start. Once I walked out into the country, on a cold spring morning. I was looking ahead from my own human perspective and foresaw huge cashflow problems. 'I've had enough, Lord,' I prayed. 'I'd rather die than go on like this. It's miserable.' And I walked amongst the graves in the cold cemetery, envying the souls peacefully at rest there.

Like Elijah, I was a prey to harassing fears. And fear is evil, since fear destroys hope. It's at the root of unbelief, since fear is evidence of an absence of trust in God's promise.

But the Lord dealt kindly with me, engendering patience in me while trade built up, at first gradually and then very quickly, as spring turned into summer. The Lord wanted me to experience at first hand how 'perfect love drives out all fear' (1 John 4:18).

It was a good thing for Elijah that his desolate prayer remained unanswered. God had something much better in store for him. Elijah prayed to be allowed to die in loneliness and apparent defeat. In reality, God was strengthening him, preparing him for the perfect plan he had made for him. In the end God transported him to glory, sweeping him up in a chariot of fire. So far from being allowed to die, he was caught up by a whirlwind into heaven!

Right from the start, God had a very special plan for Elijah. In the same way, he has a special plan for each of us. He's provided for all our needs and yet we often think we have to do things in our own strength, for ourselves. It's the survival of the fittest, we say. But if we're rooted in the true Vine, in Jesus, and he takes over our burden, then we have the fitness of God who made the world. Who can stand against us then? We are part of God's predestined love and plan. He chose us before he made the world. So we're already a part of his original blueprint. Only we ourselves can reject God's plan for us. If we've surrendered to him and his plan – and lifted up our circumstances and desires to him – then there's no stopping the outworking of that plan. He planned for us long before we were born:

> Even before the world was made, God had already chosen us to be his through our union with Christ, so that we would be holy and without fault before him.
>
> *(Eph. 1:4)*

Holy. That means *dedicated.* Dedicated to God for a special purpose.

When God told Jeremiah the prophet that he would have to go with the captive Jews into Babylon, he added: 'I alone know the plans I have for you, plans to bring you prosperity and not disaster, plans to bring about the future you hope for' (Jer.29:11). And so the years of suffering in Babylon were part of God's plan – for Jeremiah and for the Jews. It was preparing them for a future, developing hope, which is part of faith – a deliberate determination to believe, to reach out for something that could be visualised only in the mind.

Your circumstances right now might be ideal for engendering hope and belief. That's why they're part of God's plan for you. They'll begin to work for you as soon as you acknowledge to God that they're part of his plan, and praise him for them.

Don't worry if your circumstances seem hopeless. You're not seeing with God's eyes!

Let me illustrate the point.

There was a nasty crack in the wallpaper in my hotel. It ran all the way up, vertically, beneath an archway that led to the second-floor landing. It had been caused by the paper drying out after water had leaked through the roof during the building alterations. The paper had dried nicely, but must have cracked when it dried and stretched. The rest of the expensive wallpaper in the hall was undamaged. Surely it would be foolish and unnecessary to replace *all* the paper, for the sake of eliminating the unsightly crack? In any case, the style and type of wallpaper had been discontinued, so one couldn't buy just one roll.

Perhaps I could hang some large oil paintings over the crack, I thought. Or some porcelain plates?

Then it came to me: place some sort of vertical border frieze over the length of the blemish.

I found a lovely pattern on a spare sheet of wallpaper, with vertical rows of embossed blue urns. I cut out a strip from the wallpaper and glued it over the length of the crack. The effect was beautiful, for the design perfectly matched the style and colour of the decor! Then I realised that the strip was a perfect background to highlight three Wedgwood plates which, in time, I hung there, one above the other.

That little corner in the hall in a curve of the stairway became a talking point. It was one of the loveliest spots in the house! Had the blemish never happened, the beauty would never have materialised.

Now, that's exactly how the Lord, in his loving kindness, embellishes and perfects our lives. Not only does he eliminate the blemish, when we hand our lives to him, but he incorporates it into his plan for us. Our mistakes, accidents, wrong decisions, are departure points for an improved plan. So, we can surely praise and thank God for any condition or event in our lives, whether pleasant or unpleasant: either way, it's an opportunity for the Lord's grace and power.

If God, our Senior Partner, is acknowledged to be in charge, he will certainly work out all things to our good. This applies even to misfortunes. As Merlin Carothers says so aptly in *Power in Praise*: 'When we fully entrust an evil situation or condition to God, thanking and praising Him for it, the power of God will change, override, or overcome the intention and plan of the evil power inherent in the situation, transforming it to fit in with the original, perfect intention and plan of God.'

All one has to do is set one's will, in the same way that one sets the sights of a rifle. When I did cadet training at school, the master in charge of the shooting range used to keep an eye on the target with his field glasses. He used to shout out instructions after each shot: 'One notch to the left! Two notches down!' And I, lying on my stomach with the rifle under my arm, would adjust the sights on the barrel accordingly. At length I'd get it just right and hit the target in the bull's eye!

We can set our will in the same way, and hit the target. God will help us set our will. Sometimes this will mean ignoring our feelings. We won't be able to set our will correctly if we feel we're going to fail. Sometimes we need to will ourselves to love someone who has wronged us; sometimes our circumstances, or an illness, may depress us so much that we find it difficult to set our will. But *will* operates independently of feelings. Believe, without doubting, and keep your eyes off the troubled or adverse circumstances. Praise the Lord, anyway, and believe his promise.

That's what I had to do after I had overspent and overcapitalised in upgrading my hotel. The electrical contractor sent me a bill that was *thirteen times* the amount of his original quotation. The amount he wanted was enough to buy a small car! I simply didn't have the money. Also, there was no money left, after paying the other contractors, to pay the steep architect's bill. And we still had two or three months to go before the new season, when our cashflow would restart!

I was faced with the prospect of financial ruin.

Fortunately, Jo and I didn't panic. We realised that now the time had come to walk on water – like Peter climbing out of the boat and walking towards his Lord.

We had planned carefully and thought we'd avoided this kind of crisis. We hadn't bargained on actually having to walk on water, putting one step ahead of the other, one at a time, not knowing each day where our money was to come from. Each day we checked our bank balance, to be sure we weren't overdrawn – yet.

One night I read in Paul's second letter to the Corinthians: 'We should like you, our brothers, to know something of what we went through in Asia. At that time we were completely overwhelmed; the burden was more than we could bear; in fact we told ourselves that this was the end. *Yet we believe now that we had this experience of coming to the end of our tether that we might learn to trust, not in ourselves, but in God*' (II Cor.1:8-9 Phillips).

Paul and his companions were at the end of their tether because they were being persecuted for Christ. I was near the end of my financial tether. Not the same thing – but a circumstance that equally called for total dependence on and trust in God!

That night I prayed in earnest: 'Thank you, Lord, for our present financial circumstances – for now we have to trust you fully; now we have to walk on water, stepping out in faith and confidence and in your strength alone. Like the eagle nudging its young out of the nest, making it leap in faith and find its wings, you are nudging us. We praise you, Lord, for your loving kindness, and for these circumstances that activate your loving kindness and strength. We praise you for your everlasting arms around us and below us.'

As much as you may not wish it, I believe God brings you to the point where, for your own good, you have to step out in faith and walk on water. My own self-sufficiency counted for nothing. So, the more trying the circumstances, the more we will realise the true strength and power of God's strength dwelling and growing in us. Unbelief *must* be banished if we are to reach out in faith and reach our Christ-centred goal. Now, like Peter, I had to keep my eyes on Jesus and avert them from the troubled sea and brewing storm. Any doubt, even in the form of grumbling and complaining, had to be banished. I was tempted to complain and grumble about the exorbitant, unpredicted costs. I had to set my mind on the Shepherd's promise that 'I should not want.' I brought the debt to the attention of my Senior Partner in prayer. I didn't have to plead, since I had a right to approach him and ask for anything. He had said so: 'If you ask for anything in my name, I will do it' (John 14:14).

Then I thanked him and praised him that this matter was in his hands.

Thanks and praise constitute an active response to what we *know* God has done. And each day I arose with a reassuring sense of peace. Normally, I would have been fretting dreadfully. But anxiety and fear, I knew, were at the heart of unbelief. I was interested to see how God would deal with the situation, or how he would lead me to deal with it. It was even exciting, to see how God's perfect plan for me was going to unfold! In any case, whatever happened, I had set my mind, or my will, to rejoice in my trials.

Now, I expected some reasonably rational strategies from the Lord, and I left these open to him. I bought a few premium bonds, in case he liked to choose this method of supply! I entered a few competitions. And, of course, I ensured that I was open for business, since I expected him to increase my cashflow.

Fair enough, he did. Increase my cashflow, I mean. My turnover for March and April was double what it was for the same months the previous year. The A.A. representative was particularly surprised when I mentioned this. After all, she pointed out, we were in the middle of a recession. The aftermath of the Gulf War had also discouraged American visitors. I had spoken to other hoteliers: worst spring in 35 years! Well, this was only my second year, and so far my turnover was double what I experienced the previous year. Praise the Lord! Easter came, and brought in double what it brought in the year before. The previous year the trade had stopped after Easter, for a month. But this time it just kept on coming! We went to the annual Scottish Tourist Board meeting locally one day, exhausted from having served meals and cleaned rooms. The other hotel owners were there, looking fresh and immaculate. 'You're late!' they exclaimed. 'We've been working!' we said. 'You mean you had *guests*?' they asked, amazed.

Well, as I said, the additional cashflow might have been expected. What I didn't expect was the magic-wand treatment. What I would call multiplication through transubstantiation, for want of a better term. It's that dimension of the Lord's power that's extra-terrestrial, that makes him what he is – God. If he stuck to rational strategies, one might shrug one's shoulders, in the end, and dismiss the whole thing as a freak accident. The human mind always wants to rationalise and explain away miracles. Indeed, I've caught myself saying to Jo, 'It's not surprising our trade's better: after all, it shows just how much more effective our advertising is this year!'

So, explain this one away, the Lord said – and we became increasingly aware that the bank balance of our business account was *substantially higher* than it should be.

Now, I should explain that Jo, who kept a running account of our banking, was particularly careful and meticulous about how much money we had or didn't have. So, for some little while, we felt it strange that the bank balance was increasing rather dramatically faster than it should have been. Strange, too, since we had just paid out a steady stream of cash – electricity bills, telephone bills, advertising costs, and suchlike. But every time Jo checked our balance, the gap between what we had and what we should have had widened – very much in our favour. Then all of our books were handed over to our accountant for the annual accounting and tax assessment. Before long the accountant phoned us: 'You've more than a thousand pounds in your business account that I can account for,' he said. 'We know!' we said.

In short, neither we, nor the accountant, could trace the source of those extra funds. They were just *there*.

Then the architect's bill arrived. It was for £1, 700 – rather less than we had anticipated! And it dawned on us that we had more than enough funds to pay it.

Furthermore, our joiner, the chief contractor, had been dragging his heels in the submission of the final accounts for his work. So much time lapsed that, as it turned out, the additional funds for paying him were available by the time his bill arrived - by the end of May. At the worst we expected to carry an overdraft well into the summer - but all year we kept above water, praising the Lord! And this principle of walking on water, praising God and going ahead in faith, step by step, was the basis of our development in the years that followed. A year later our turnover had tripled; we purchased a country cottage in delightful open countryside, and the following year acquired a Victorian town house across the road. Somehow, the Lord's supply was always replenished, and always there to meet our need.

This phenomenon of 'multiplication through transubstantiation' is very intriguing, isn't it? The Catholics use the word *transubstantiation* to explain a phenomenon in the Eucharist, at the moment when the wine is instantly transformed into the actual physical substance of the Lord's blood.

Perhaps I'm misusing the word, in view of its specific application to the Lord's blood. But since it refers to a process that seems magic (in the Catholic context, at the sound of a bell rung by the priest), it best describes the phenomenon for me.

What evidence is there in the Bible of this sort of multiplying transubstantiatory power? Something of this might have happened, of course, when the Lord turned the water into wine. What he did came as a complete surprise. Something similar might have happened when he filled his disciples' boat with fishes. Of course, when the disciples told him they had toiled all night and taken nothing, he didn't fill the boat with fishes without effort on their part. His command was: 'Launch out into the deep and let down your nets for a draught.' In so far as they didn't doubt or worry, and were obedient in carrying out his instructions, they were co-partners in enabling the supply. This sort of co-operation might have been evident when I made sure my hotel was ready for business, when I put out the menus in the bedrooms, hauled up the St Andrews cross to the top of the flagstaff in the front of the hotel, and waited for the rooms to fill. But *financial transubstantiation* – what kind of co-operation from me was expected for the Lord to do *that?* Complete trust and expectation, yes. But that's as far as my co-operation was possible. I could hardly expect what followed. It goes to show how we mustn't dictate to God how to perform his work, or tell him how he must answer our prayers. He is, after all, God, and his ways are inscrutable and considerably above ours, and beyond our understanding. We mustn't limit God!

Come to think of it, it's one of the reasons we love him! Because he's mysterious – and, like a loving father, he likes to surprise us!

Surprise us – like he did when he multiplied the loaves and fishes. Now *that* was what I call multiplication by transubstantiation! All he had was five small barley loaves and two small fishes in a basket – and it was enough to feed *five thousand!* (John 6:1-13: the leftovers alone filled twelve baskets!)

Something similar happened many years before – when the prophet Elijah was fed by the widow at Zarephath. It took the widow by surprise, too – for she didn't know that, in first feeding Elijah from her meagre store of flour and oil, that both articles would literally increase and fail to run out. She had enough for days, feeding not only Elijah but herself and her child, too, in a time of famine. You can read all about it in chapter 17 of the First Book of Kings. She only had a handful of flour in a jar and a little oil in a jug. At first she refused to feed Elijah, saying she barely had enough for herself and her child. In fact, her attitude was quite negative since she expected to die in the famine anyway. But Elijah reassured her, telling her not to be anxious. (Is that the key? Don't be anxious – trust completely!) First she had to use some of the flour and oil to make some bread for Elijah. ('Seek ye first the kingdom of God, and all these things will be added unto you...') She found Elijah's words literally came true:

> 'The jar of flour will not be used up and the jug of
> oil will not dry until the day the Lord gives rain on
> the land.'

So – there was food every day for Elijah and the woman and her family! Multiplication through transubstantiation – or whatever process it is!

The important lesson is that God leads and multiplies. We'll only experience his uncanny power of multiplication if we allow him to lead, and follow his leadership – a response that involves our effort – our trust and our obedience. He must go before, and we must follow, trusting, like children. It's as though Jesus were saying to us: 'Once you are born of the Spirit, that is your life's breath. You must never doubt, never worry, but step by step, the way to freedom must be trodden. See that you walk it with me.' The Lord goes before, preparing the way – for us to bless and be blessed. As I said, miraculous living is a result of a partnership with Christ. It's adventurous living, since we're blessed with the joy that comes from delighting in his love. Through it, we can claim big things. We can claim joy and peace and freedom from care. As partners with Christ, we're in a privileged position. If we're partners, this is what he says to us: 'I am your Senior Partner, yes. But I am your Lord, your Creator, too. Remember that I am the same yesterday, today and for ever. Your Creator, when I called the world into being. Your Creator, too, when, today, by loving thought of you, I call into being all you need on the material plane. Keep the eye of your spirit ever upon me, the window of your soul open towards me. You have ever to know that all things are yours – that what is lovely I delight to give you. So empty your mind of all that limits. Whatever is beautiful you can have. Leave more and more the choice to me. You will have no regrets.'

Partnership is trusting and sharing. It works both ways, of course. But often it's the Lord, in his mercy and loving kindness, who does most of the sharing!

The important thing I had to remember, and which I kept reminding myself, was to keep my mind positive, rejoicing, tuned to praise. The attitude of praise releases the power of God into our lives, but the attitude of worry, anxiety, often expressed in murmuring or complaining, blocks that power. Carothers points out that by complaining we are actually accusing God of mismanaging the details of our day. And, after all, I had placed all of my life, with every daily routine, into God's hands.

Jesus said, sufficient unto the day is the evil thereof. That meant, it wasn't necessary for me to worry about how I was going to pay my debt in the long term: all I had to do was cross each bridge as I came to it on a daily basis. And that was easy! Each morning I awoke and spoke to the Lord. He sent peace into my heart, and I had abundant strength to deal with any problem that needed solving *on that day.*

Don't jump the gun and try to take things out of God's hands, having placed them in his hands, by worrying about things in advance! That was the lesson God was teaching me: each day was a new step on the water. No need to run ahead: just take one step at a time, and *keep your eyes on Jesus.* Jesus is the source of power and strength, and will readily help you and pull you up, if you do find yourself beginning to sink.

In our daily dependence on God, we need to keep the channel open between him and ourselves. This is particularly true, too, if we are to be channels of his love, joy and laughter in this still imperfect world. My prayer is that through this little book my experiences in keeping the channel open with God and venturing out in faith will bring confidence and joy to *you.*

In keeping the channel open as we discover and reach out for our goal, I'm reminded of Captain Picard's words in the TV *Star Trek* series; almost every time his exploratory 'away' team is beamed down to a strange and dangerous planet, he transmits the order: 'Keep this channel open'; or, 'Maintain an open frequency!' This expresses his concern for his team: he wants to monitor the team members' words and actions, so he can transmit his counsel urgently if needed, or give the order to beam them up quickly if they fall into danger.

We have a living God that speaks to us today, who plans and guides us, who rescues us out of danger. No detail is too insignificant for his attention. He reveals himself now as ever as a loving Father or, if you like, as a loving Captain who likes to monitor our strategies and our actions and our thoughts for our own good. It helps if we maintain an open frequency with him. An open channel will also ensure the ready inflow of his love and power, as he upholds us and enables us to conquer great odds as we fulfil our most cherished dreams.

In the end we'll find that our dreams are the very dreams God put in our hearts in the first place. His perfect plan for us will have been revealed and fulfilled.

APPENDIX

A Tarnished Cup in the Attic

It was in the bleak December of 2011 while I was staying, alone, at my home in Clashnessie, in the remote north-western Highlands of Scotland where the coastline was being ravaged by gales and freezing rain and sleet, that I realised how a seemingly insignificant decision in the past had completely altered the course of my life. I was searching through boxes in the attic, looking for copies of my book *Fiction Studies* that was published some years ago by McGraw-Hill while I was Professor and Head of the Department of English at the University of the North in

South Africa, when I came across a very tarnished silver cup, or chalice. It was almost black with oxidation, but I could just make out the words engraved on it: "Charles H Muller, Mathematics, 1962."

After a precursory glance I threw it back into the box where it had lain forgotten for the past five years. It was a meaningless cup, really, that didn't prove or celebrate any significant achievement, for at school I was hopeless at mathematics. It was sent to me by Union College, a correspondence college in Johannesburg, simply because I had enrolled for their matriculation course in 1961, my final school year.

Then it hit me. If it were not for that course in mathematics, I would not be where I was now. I would not have become a Professor of English, I would not have achieved seven university degrees, including three doctorates; and I would not have been awarded an overseas research bursary that took me to America and England, where I met my wife in Yorkshire in 1977, and, consequently, would not have had my five precious children, including my youngest son who graduated from the University of St Andrews, first class, with a Master of Mathematics degree (with the Duncan prize for the best student in his Honours year), and who went on to study for his MSc degree in Artificial Intelligence at Edinburgh University, and thereafter to a PhD at York University.

The realisation was like an epiphany. I picked up the tarnished cup again, holding it in my hands, almost with a sense of reverence. "My God," I said to nobody in particular, "this cup has changed my life!" I took it downstairs and got some stove polish and, sitting in front of a blazing log fire in the wood-burning stove, rubbed the metal until the cup shone again, like new. I mulled over the importance of that mathematics course.

1960 was my penultimate year at school – at Grey College, in Bloemfontein, the second oldest school in South Africa. In the preliminary end-of-year examinations I had failed almost half of my subjects. The report card showed a red ring around each failed subject, and one of them was maths. At about the same time I was asked by Mr Eddie East, my form teacher, for my English homework. I confessed that I had not done it. He drew himself up into a towering rage: "You might as well leave school and go to the Tech, Muller! Learn to do something with your hands because you will never do anything with your brain!"

Eddie East was like a sergeant major, and one went to school in fear and trembling at evoking his rage, so I am surprised that I had taken the risk of ignoring my homework. Nevertheless, that particular outburst, for once, really struck home. It was time for me to wake up! Clearly I had little hope of passing that year (we called it Standard Nine), and if I failed I would not be promoted to Standard Ten, or "Matric", the final school year. I became very conscious, too, that the final Matric examinations would decide whether I was qualified for an entrance into university. My head was in the clouds, those days – I wanted to be an astronaut; or failing that, an astronomer; or failing that, at least an academic of some kind. But here I was, faced with almost certain failure, and I knew that the prospect of passing mathematics at the end of that year was hopeless. I could apply myself to the other subjects, like Geography and Science and Biology – but mathematics! I simply could not get my head around fractions, algebra and geometry. So there was only one recourse – to drop mathematics at this, the eleventh hour, and take an easier subject, if only to avoid failing the year. So I dropped it and was allowed to take commerce in its place—which proved to be an easy subject, learning about co-operative societies and the principles of retail. The main objective, at the time, was simply to get into that last school-leaving year. Once there I could address the matter of mathematics, somehow, because I was aware that I would still need to pass matric maths to gain the school leaving certificate with "matriculation exemption" that would qualify me to be accepted by a university for degree study.

So I applied myself and wrote the end of year exams, and this time there were no red circles around any of the results—and I was promoted to the Matric year, the final year at school. In Matric the boys were allowed to wear a boater straw hat they called a "Cheesecutter" as part of the uniform. It showed you were a cut above the rest, as it were! I was away on holiday with my cousins in Johannesburg when the report card arrived, and my mother, following my instructions if I had passed, sent me a telegram that read, "Congratulations Cheesecuter" (spelt with one 't' but never mind, the message was clear and I breathed a sigh of relief).

Having got over the hurdle of getting into the final year, I had to find a way of securing that matriculation exemption qualification. To achieve that, one of my subjects had to be a third language like German or Latin – or Mathematics. There was no question of tackling a third language at this late stage, given that in less than a year I would have to write the examination. (English and Afrikaans were the compulsory first and second languages, which I now had under control.) That is why I enrolled, at my own expense, for the Union College matric mathematics course – to bring myself up to speed in maths so I could write it as an additional subject when I presented myself for the matric exams at the end of the year. I paid for the course by saving up my pocket money. The course was a struggle – there were no classes to attend and everything was done by correspondence. Nearer to the end of the year I found a retired maths teacher with a very gentle and caring disposition, Mr Dixon, who agreed to tutor me and with him I worked through previous exam papers. He told me to learn my theorems well, and focus on what I could do, like the theorems and graphs before attempting the algebraic and trigonometry problems. If I could just achieve 33.3%....!

And I did! My classmates and schoolteachers were surprised when I presented myself for the mathematics paper, and when the results were published in the Government Gazette, the pages pasted up in glass cases in front of the city hall, I looked eagerly through the lists to see if my name was there accompanied by the all-important asterisk which would tell me that I had passed with matriculation exemption – and my name was there, *with* the asterisk! I still think that was the most rewarding and exciting moment in my life.

Dawie Marquard, my old maths teacher who was there, sitting on the steps of the government buildings, saw me and asked, "Did you pass maths, Muller?"

"Yes sir!" I beamed.

The cup bears the date of 1962, which was my first year at the University of Natal, in Pietermaritzburg, where I was engaged in study for the B.A. degree. I can't remember now, but I think I must have bought it retrospectively, as a monument to my determination and achievement in the preceding year. In any case, my mother was so impressed by my success, and by my initiative in using my pocket money to enrol in the Union College course, that she refunded the cost of the course in full – bless her. I used the money she gave me for a correspondence course in Pelmanism, which was a training exercise in positive thinking and achievement of goals. The lesson is clear, I think – never undervalue the importance of making a decision, and sticking to it.

C.H.M.

About the Author

Charles Humphrey Muller, MA (Wales), PhD (London), D.Litt (UFS), D.Ed (SA), was Professor and Head of the Department of English at the University of the North (now University of Limpopo) in South Africa for ten years, and Senior Lecturer in English at the University of South Africa before that. He is the author of numerous academic textbooks and literary studies published by Oxford University Press, McGraw-Hill and Macmillan, and was editor of *Unisa English Studies* and *Communiqué*, literary journals of the University of South Africa and the University of the North. In 1988 he left his academic career to move to Scotland where he bought a small hotel – the Kenmore Bank Hotel in Jedburgh, fifty miles south of Edinburgh – which he and his wife Joanne ran for eleven years. During this time he founded his editing and publishing business, Diadem Books. He has since written a number of novels (*A Slip in Time,*

Release of the Dove, Wheel of Destiny, An Elusive Sanctuary, and under the pen name of Callum Gunn, *Circle of Deceit*). With his wife Joanne he co-authored two novels (*Ocean Rapture* and *Spirit of Joy*). He wrote the inspirational work *Steps to Success* and served as editor for his wife's 'self-help' book *So You Want to Buy a Small Hotel!* He also edited a collection of testimonies titled *Touched by Angels.* After selling his hotel in Jedburgh in 2001, he has lived in the Great Glen of Scotland, Clashnessie in Sutherland, in Nova Scotia (Canada), in New Zealand, and the Kingdom of Fife—locales that feature in his travel memoirs, *Waipori Reflections*: *Contemplations in Three Locations.* He published many of his autobiographical memories under the title *Bragleenbeg Reflections*, and recently republished his academic study of Charles Kingsley: *The Christian Teachings of Charles Kingsley*. More recently he moved to Spain where he continues to write and where he has retired as CEO of Diadem Books.

www.ingramcontent.com/pod-product-compliance
Lightning Source LLC
Chambersburg PA
CBHW030816180526
45163CB00003B/1305